# THE GOSPEL OF LUKE

## THE BRIDGE BIBLE
*Connecting the Biblical to the Contemporary World*

© 2020 by Ryan Baltrip
All rights reserved. No part of this book may be reproduced in any form without permission in writing from the publisher, except in the case of brief quotations embodied in critical articles or reviews.
ebook ISBN: 978-0-9980333-2-7
paperback ISBN: 978-0-9980333-3-4

# CONTENTS

1. **Understanding God's plan: Discover how He has worked throughout history to provide a path of salvation for all people through Jesus Christ (1:1–4)** .......................... 1

   **LUKE CHAPTER 1** | page 1

2. **Fulfilling God's plan of salvation: God has worked throughout human history to bring Jesus into the world and make His salvation available to all through Him (1:5–2:52)** ................ 2

    2.1. Announcing the Savior: Understand the scope of the salvation Jesus brings (1:5—80).

        2.1.1 Before he is born, an angel announces that John the Baptist will prepare everyone for a new era of human existence, which Jesus will bring. John will be a herald of that coming salvation (1:5–25).

        2.1.2 Before He is born, an angel announces that Jesus will be the One who brings salvation to God's people—the King who will bring perfect harmony and community to all people and all things through His kingdom rule (1:26–38).

    2.2. Defining the Savior's work: Understand that Jesus is the One who fulfills God's plan to make salvation available to all (1:39—80).

        2.2.1 God has worked throughout human history to make salvation available to everyone through Jesus Christ (1:39–56)

        2.2.2 God has worked throughout human history to make salvation available to all, and John the Baptist is a prophet who will prepare people for the arrival of God's salvation through Christ (1:57–80).

    2.3. Celebrating the Savior's arrival: The Savior is born, and heaven celebrates the peace He will bring to the earth (2:1–21).

   **LUKE CHAPTER 2** | page 9

    2.4. Discovering the Savior: The newborn Savior of the world is recognized as the One who fulfills God's work of salvation throughout history (2:22–40)

2.5. Discovering the Savior: The Savior of the world is fully human but knows, throughout His life, that He is serving and fulfilling God's plan of salvation (2:41–52).

3. **Clarifying God's plan of salvation: Jesus demonstrates that He is qualified to represent both humanity and God's people as the Messiah, the One who will bring salvation (3:1–4:13). . . . . . . 14**

   3.1. John the Baptist makes it clear: One must decide to follow Jesus and make a clear, conscious commitment to following Him or suffer the consequences before God (3:1-20).

**LUKE CHAPTER 3 | page 14**

   3.2. God makes it clear: Jesus is God's Son who will reveal His truth and salvation to the world (3:21–22).

   3.3. The history of God's work makes it clear: Jesus fulfills God's promises to His people and is the One who brings salvation to all (3:23–38).

   3.4. Jesus' actions make it clear: Jesus resists the devil's temptation and does not deviate from God's plan to make salvation available to all (4:1–13).

**LUKE CHAPTER 4 | page 20**

4. **Recognizing the Savior: Will people recognize who Jesus is? [The Galilean Ministry] (4:14–9:50). . . . . . . . . . . . . . . . . . . . . . . . 21**

   4.1. Jesus demonstrates who He is through His powerful teaching and actions (4: 14–44).

      4.1.1. Jesus' teaching conveys the divine truth He came to reveal to the world (4:14–30).

      4.1.2 Jesus' actions reflect the divine compassion He came to reveal to the world (4:31–44).

   4.2. Jesus introduces a new era with a new way of God working in the world, one that will transform lives and encounters opposition to God's plan (5:1–6:16).

      4.2.1. Jesus transforms lives as He calls people to follow Him and demonstrates His power to change people's lives (5:1–32).

**LUKE CHAPTER 5 | page 26**

      4.2.2. Jesus introduces a new era of God's work and a new way of God working in the world (5:33–6:5).

**LUKE CHAPTER 6 | page 31**

      4.2.3 Jesus encounters opposition to His authority and the new way of God working in the world (6:6–16).

### 4.3. Jesus teaches a new way, a new pattern of living for God (6:17–49).

    4.3.1. Jesus identifies those who are truly fortunate before God and those who are not (6:20-26).

    4.3.2. Jesus teaches about showing love, mercy, and hesitation to judge others (6:27-38).

    4.3.3. Jesus teaches about living right with God, bearing the fruit of one's faith, and building one's life on a wise foundation (6:39-49).

### 4.4. Jesus shows that faith in Him is the way to experience salvation (7:1–8:3).

    4.4.1. Jesus demonstrates that faith in Him has the authority to heal and that He has power over all things, even death (7:1–17).

## LUKE CHAPTER 7 | page 38

    4.4.2. Jesus teaches that faith in Him is the way to God's salvation, not trusting in social, political, or military power (7:18–35).

    4.4.3. Jesus identifies that a humble, trusting faith in Him is the way to experience God's forgiveness, not following the legalistic letter of religious teachings (7:36–8:3).

## LUKE CHAPTER 8 | page 44

### 4.5. Jesus shows what faith in Him looks like by calling on His disciples to trust in Him and His Word (8:4–9:17).

    4.5.1 Jesus teaches that people must respond to His Word with faith (8:4–21).

    4.5.2. Jesus teaches that His followers can trust Him to care for their best interests, no matter what storms may come in their lives, and that He has power and authority over nature [Miracle 1: The Stilling of the Storm] (8:22–25).

    4.5.3. Jesus teaches how people can have a variety of responses to Him, and that He has power and authority over demonic power [Miracle 2: Jesus exorcises demons] (8:26–39).

    4.5.4. Jesus teaches that sometimes faith needs bolstering and encouragement, while other times it needs calm, persistent trusting, and that He has power and authority over disease and death [Miracles 3 and 4: A healing and a resuscitation from the dead] (8:40–56).

    4.5.5. Jesus teaches that the message of the arrival of His kingdom is a message of hope that should be spread and shared with everyone (9:1–9).

## LUKE CHAPTER 9 | page 51

    4.5.6. Jesus teaches that He will provide for the needs of His followers (9:10–17).

### 4.6. Responding to Jesus through faith: One must confess trust in Christ and continue to live by faith in Him daily (9:18–50).

    4.6.1. Faith in Jesus requires confessing complete trust in Christ, who He is, and the salvation He brings to His people (9:18–22).

- 4.6.2. Faith in Jesus requires a continual and daily commitment to following Him (9:23–27).
- 4.6.3. Faith in Jesus requires listening to Him and recognizing the ongoing need to listen to Him (9:28–36).
- 4.6.4. Faith in Jesus requires trusting in His power at work in our lives, not relying on our means and power, and recognizing that He is calling people from all walks of life to follow and serve Him (9:37–50).

## 5. Following the Savior: The life of following Christ is a journey of faith. [The Journey to Jerusalem] (9:51–19:44). . . . . . . . . . . 57

- 5.1. The life of following Christ requires commitment and will include both moments of failure and success (9:51–10:24).
  - 5.1.1. Following Christ is not a casual affair but requires commitment (9:51–62).
  - 5.1.2. Following Christ calls one into God's service, and serving Him will include both moments of failure and success (10:1–24).

**LUKE CHAPTER 10** | page 59

- 5.2. The life of following Christ influences one's relationships with others (10:25–11:13).
  - 5.2.1. Following Christ requires seeing everyone as a neighbor who should be loved (10:25–37).
  - 5.2.2. Following Christ requires a balanced life of faith (10:38–42).
  - 5.2.3. Following Christ requires a healthy life of prayer (11:1–13).

**LUKE CHAPTER 11** | page 64

- 5.3. The life of following Christ calls for one to trust in His authority, His truth, and the light of His teaching (11:14–54).
  - 5.3.1. Following Christ calls for one to trust in Jesus' power and authority (11:14–23).
  - 5.3.2. Following Christ calls for one to make a decisive decision to trust in Him and the light of His teaching (11:24–36).
  - 5.3.3. Following Christ calls for one to trust in His truth with a heart that is not blind or hard to His teaching (11:37–54).
- 5.4. The life of following Christ requires a faithful pursuit of trusting in and serving Him with an undistracted eye (12:1–48).
  - 5.4.1. Following Christ calls one to fear harming God's reputation in the world more than fearing what others think (12:1–12).

**LUKE CHAPTER 12** | page 72

- 5.4.2. Following Christ calls one to take a proper perspective toward resources (12:13–21).
- 5.4.3. Following Christ calls one not to worry but to trust in God's

           provision for one's life (12:22–34).

      5.4.4. Following Christ calls one to be a faithful steward with the resources He has provided (12:35–48).

**5.5. The life of following Christ requires recognizing the nature and limitations of time (12:49–14:24).**

      5.5.1. Following Christ calls one to recognize that following Him can cause one to be divided from those who reject Him (12:49–13:9).

**LUKE CHAPTER 13 | page 80**

      5.5.2. Following Christ calls one to be faithful, while others refuse to respond to Him (13:10–17).

      5.5.3. Following Christ calls one to faithfully focus on His kingdom's coming while others may choose another path in life, which will lead to their own peril (13:18–35).

      5.5.4. Following Christ calls for living a life of humble faithfulness while others may or may not respond to God's work (14:1–24).

**LUKE CHAPTER 14 | page 86**

**5.6. The life of following Christ requires Jesus to be the main priority in one's life (14:25–35).**

**5.7. The life of following Christ calls one to have a compassionate heart and to seek out those who are lost (15:1–32).**

      5.7.1. Following Christ calls one to seek out those who are lost (15:1–10).

**LUKE CHAPTER 15 | page 90**

      5.7.2. Following Christ calls one to have compassion for those who are lost (15:11–32).

**5.8. The life of following Christ calls for one to be wise and generous with the resources God has given them (16:1–31).**

      5.8.1. Following Christ calls for one to faithfully use the resources that God has given them (16:1–13).

**LUKE CHAPTER 16 | page 93**

      5.8.2. Following Christ calls for one to recognize that He brings a new era of human living and trusts in Him as the source of what one values most in life (16:14–18).

      5.8.3. Following Christ calls one to be generous in meeting human needs in this life because people's decisions about Him will have eternal consequences (16:19–31).

**5.9. The life of following Christ will confront false teaching and require one to embody forgiveness, faith, and service (17:1–10).**

**LUKE CHAPTER 17 | page 98**

5.10. The life of following Christ requires one to trust in God's plan and timing, and to be faithful in looking toward the King, His Kingdom, and the ultimate consummation of His rule (17:11–18:8).

- 5.10.1. Following Christ calls for faith and gratitude, and the call to follow Him is freely available to everyone (17:11–19).
- 5.10.2. Following Christ calls one to recognize and trust in the King and the hope of His kingdom that is present in His presence (17:20–18:8).

**LUKE CHAPTER 18** | page 103

5.11. The life of following Christ requires faithful humility and trusting in the Father for all things in life (18:9–30).

- 5.11.1. Following Christ calls one to live a faithful life of humility before God (18:9–17).
- 5.11.2. Following Christ calls for one to follow the example of a child, to have a simple, trusting, and humble faith in the Heavenly Father (18:15-17).
- 5.11.3. Following Christ calls for one to trust in the Father above all other things in one's life (18:18–30).

5.12. The life of following Christ requires faith and calls for one to trust in God's plan (18:31–19:44).

- 5.12.1 Following Christ calls one to look for and see what God is doing even if one's expectations are different or if one is slow to see His work; a blind man can see what no one else does (18:31–43)
- 5.12.2. Following Christ calls one to recognize that He has come to seek and offer salvation to everyone (19:1–10).

**LUKE CHAPTER 19** | page 108

- 5.12.3. Following Christ calls one to a life of faithful service and stewardship under His rule and within His kingdom (19:11–27).
- 5.12.4. Following Christ calls one to follow a humble King who fulfills God's plan and rules a different kind of kingdom (19:28–44).

6. **Discovering the Savior's victory: Jesus fulfills God's plan to make salvation available to all through His innocent suffering and by His vindication through His resurrection [In Jerusalem] (19:45–24:53). . . . . . . . . . . . . . . . . . . . . . . . . . . . . . . . . . . . . . . .113**

- 6.1. Hold onto the truth: Even though Jesus is challenged, questioned, and surrounded in controversy by human beings who do not understand Him, God is fulfilling His plan to bring salvation to the world (19:45–21:4).
  - 6.1.1. Jesus is challenged about the source of His authority (19:45–20:8).

**LUKE CHAPTER 20** | page 114

- 6.1.2. Jesus challenges people's perspective on how they view the history of

- God's work and activity in the world (20:9–19).
  - 6.1.3. Jesus is challenged by a plot against Him and remains innocent when overcoming a politically incriminating trap (20:20–26).
  - 6.1.4. Jesus addresses questions on the afterlife and resurrection (20:27–40).
  - 6.1.5. Jesus challenges His accusers with a theological question about the identity of the Messiah that they cannot answer (20:41–44).
  - 6.1.6. Jesus provides a final warning about the need to respond to His truth by contrasting one wrong way (led by personal pride in accomplishment) and one right way (led by personal humility in generous giving) (20:45–21:4).

## LUKE CHAPTER 21 | page 119

- **6.2. Be informed and encouraged: The old ways are broken and will come to a devastating end, but God is bringing a new way to be right with Him, which will be available to all people; keep one's eyes open, God's victory is coming through Christ (21:5–38).**
  - 6.2.1. The old way is broken; a devastating end will come to it (21:5-19).
  - 6.2.2. The old center of religious life will shift from a building to a person (21:20:24).
  - 6.2.3. The old way of religious life is ending, but it is not the end of the story; God's kingdom is coming to the world in a new way (21:25-28).
  - 6.2.4. The old way of religious life is ending; one should keep their eyes open to see what God is doing and be ready for the end (21:29-38).
- **6.3. Recognize the betrayal of the innocent Jesus; realize His vindication is coming; and remember His teaching when His victory and vindication have been achieved (22:1–38).**
  - 6.3.1. Jesus, the innocent One who is fulfilling God's plan for salvation, is betrayed (22:1–6).

## LUKE CHAPTER 22 | page 124

  - 6.3.2. Jesus' vindication is coming; remember His sacrifice when it has been achieved (22:7–20).
  - 6.3.3. Jesus' vindication is coming; remember His teaching when it has been achieved (22:21–38).
- **6.4. Recognize that Jesus's innocent suffering is part of God's plan for fulfilling His plan to make salvation available to all (22:39–23:56).**
  - 6.4.1. Jesus, the innocent One sent from God, prepares for His suffering through prayer (22:39–46).
  - 6.4.2. Jesus, the innocent One sent from God, is betrayed and arrested (22:47–53).
  - 6.4.3. Jesus, the innocent One sent from God, stands trial while His followers deny Him (22:54–71).

6.4.4. Jesus, the innocent One sent from God, stands trial before Pilate and Herod; His innocence is on full display (23:1–12).

**LUKE CHAPTER 23** | page 131

6.4.5. Jesus, the innocent One sent from God, is rejected and condemned to death instead of a person who is fully guilty; His rejection in order to fulfill God's plan of salvation has been completed (23:13–25).

6.4.6. Jesus, the innocent One sent from God, is crucified and dies; His sacrifice in order to fulfill God's plan of salvation has been completed (23:26–49).

6.4.7. Jesus, the innocent One sent from God, is buried; His suffering in order to fulfill God's plan of salvation has been completed (23:50–56).

**6.5. Realize that through the victory of Jesus' resurrection and ascension, God fulfills His plan and makes salvation available to the world (24:1-53).**

6.5.1. Jesus' resurrection fulfills God's plan of salvation and achieves His vindication and victory (24:1–12).

**LUKE CHAPTER 24** | page 136

6.5.2. Jesus' resurrection fulfills God's plan of salvation and delights those who follow Him and the truth of His teaching (24:13–35).

6.5.3. Jesus' resurrection fulfills God's plan of salvation; before He ascends, He gives a promise to hold onto and a commission that they must fulfill (24:36–53).

# LUKE

1. Understanding God's plan: Discover how He has worked throughout history to provide a path of salvation for all people through Jesus Christ (1:1–4).

**CHAPTER 1**

¹Many people have set out to produce faithful narratives about Christ. They desired to communicate all the things Christ accomplished and fulfilled while living among us. ²These people were servants of God's Word who knew how to handle the truth; they handed down God's Word that had been given to them with great care. They produced their faithful narratives from original eyewitness reports. ³In a similar fashion, I have decided to write a faithful narrative for you, most honorable Theophilus, that you, as a God-fearing person, might better understand God's plan of salvation, which He has been working throughout history to accomplish through Christ. The narrative I write has been produced after carefully investigating everything. I have traced and tracked everything from the very beginning so that I may write a clear, logical, and orderly narrative about Christ Jesus. ⁴I have produced this faithful account so that you may be certain that everything you have been taught is true, that what you believe is reliable, and that you may know you fit into God's plan.

Now, let us start this orderly and faithful narrative about Christ; let us start at the beginning with the announcement of His arrival.

2. Fulfilling God's plan of salvation: God has worked throughout human history to bring Jesus into the world and make His salvation available to all through Him (1:5–2:52).

> 2.1. Announcing the Savior: Understand the scope of the salvation Jesus brings (1:5—80).
>
>> 2.1.1 Before he is born, an angel announces that John the Baptist will prepare everyone for a new era of human existence, which Jesus will bring. John will be a herald of that coming salvation (1:5–25).

⁵During the time when Herod was king of Judea, there was a priest named Zechariah. Zechariah was one of around 18,000 Jewish priests; he belonged to the priestly division of Abijah and served in the Temple for one week, two times per year. Zechariah's wife was Elizabeth, and she was descended from the daughters of Aaron. ⁶Both Zechariah and Elizabeth lived righteous, honorable lives in God's eyes. They faithfully observed all the Lord's commands and directions. ⁷However, even though they lived upright lives, they were childless because Elizabeth was not able to conceive; they both were very old.

⁸One day, Zechariah's priestly division was on duty in the Temple, and he was serving as the priest making the daily sacrifice before God. This duty was a unique, once-in-a-lifetime experience. A priest was only allowed to officiate the sacrifice before God in the Temple once in his life. ⁹It was customary for the priest making the sacrifice each day to be chosen by casting dice. Zechariah was chosen in this manner, and on this day, he entered into the temple of the Lord, which symbolized the place where God lived. Inside the temple of the Lord, he burned incense to God as an act of cleansing the people of Israel from their sin. ¹⁰While the incense was being burned inside, a vast multitude of worshipers gathered outside to pray collectively to God.

¹¹Zechariah was engaged in the most important moment of his career, but more than that, it was a deeply meaningful moment. He was

burning incense as a sacrifice to God on behalf of all Israel's sins, an act dedicated to people collectively recognizing their need to be cleansed from sin. As Zechariah was engaged in this special moment, an angel of the Lord appeared to him, standing to the right side of the incense altar. [12]When Zechariah saw him, he was overwhelmed with fear.

[13]But the angel of the Lord calmed his fear and said, "Do not be afraid, Zechariah. God has heard your prayer. Your wife, Elizabeth, will bear a son, and you are to name him John. [14]His birth will be a source of great joy and gladness for you. But the joy he brings will not be just for you and your wife. Many will rejoice because of his birth, [15]for John will have a very important stature in the eyes of the Lord. Since John will serve a special, divine purpose, he must take a special vow of devotion to God. As a result, he must never drink wine or other alcoholic drinks. Instead, he will be filled with a more powerful force and reality—the Holy Spirit—even before he is even born. [16]By serving God's purpose, John will turn many people of Israel back to the Lord their God. [17]But the special purpose John will serve has even bigger implications! After four hundred years of prophetic silence and having no prophetic voice, the people of Israel, the Jewish people, will hear a prophetic voice once again. John will be a prophetic voice who restores God's Word and promises to His people. In the same spirit and power as the prophet Elijah in the Old Covenant Scriptures, John will soften the callous, hard hearts of adults and turn them into the receptive, teachable hearts of children. For those who have been wholly set on living in their own disobedient, selfish ways, John will ignite a passion in them to understand and pursue godly wisdom. He will prepare everyone for a new era of human existence: the time of the Lord's arrival."

[18]Even though he was a godly man, Zechariah had doubts after hearing what the angel said. He asked, "All of this sounds amazing, but how can I know for sure it all will happen? Is there any sign you can give me to confirm it? My wife and I are old. I am not sure we can even have a child at our ages."

[19]The angel responded to him, "I am Gabriel. I stand in the very presence of God and know first-hand that He can do all things. He sent me to bring you this good news. [20]But since you have doubts, I want

you to be able to sit back and watch God do His work. So, I will give you a sign, the sign of silence. From this moment until the day your son is born, you will be silent and unable to speak. In silence, you will be able to see all of my words come true at their appointed time."

²¹As Zechariah's angelic encounter was taking place inside, the people outside the Temple were waiting on Zechariah. They wondered why he was taking so long. ²²When Zechariah finally did come out, he was not able to speak to them. He made various signs and gestures to the people, trying to let them know what had happened. While they could not understand any of the specifics, they did realize he had seen a vision while inside the Temple.

²³When Zechariah's week of service in the Temple was over, he returned to his home. ²⁴Not long after he had returned home, his wife Elizabeth became pregnant. For five months, she secluded herself so that she could delight in the blessing of her pregnancy. ²⁵She said, "The Lord has shown me incredible favor and kindness. He has taken away my personal and social disgrace of not being able to conceive and have a child."

> 2.1.2 Before He is born, an angel announces that Jesus will be the One who brings salvation to God's people—the King who will bring perfect harmony and community to all people and all things through His kingdom rule (1:26–38).

²⁶In the sixth month of Elizabeth's pregnancy, God sent the angel Gabriel to an obscure, humble Galilean village called Nazareth. ²⁷God sent Gabriel there to visit a virgin named Mary. Mary had been betrothed to a man named Joseph, who was a descendant of David. Mary's betrothal to Joseph involved a formal engagement, which included a contract agreement and a dowry (money given to the bride's family as a way of ensuring that she would be taken care of by her husband). Mary's betrothal also included a commitment to a wedding, which usually occurred a year after the engagement. ²⁸Into this context, the angel Gabriel appeared to Mary and said, "Greetings. By God's grace, special purpose, and choosing, you are highly favored! The Lord is with you."

[29] Mentally shocked and overwhelmed by the angel's presence, Mary tried to understand the meaning of this greeting. [30] But the angel of the Lord assured her, "Mary, do not be afraid. By God's grace and choosing, you are the recipient of God's goodwill and favor. [31] Now pay special attention to what I am about to tell you. You will become pregnant and give birth to a son. You are to name him Jesus. [32] He will be great and will be called the Son of the Highest Being in Existence. He will have a special relationship with the Lord God, and God will give Him the throne of his forefather David. [33] But unlike David or other kings of Israel, Jesus will fulfill God's promise of a King who will rule over Israel forever; His kingdom will never end!"

[34] Curiously, Mary asked the angel, "But how can this happen? I am a virgin and not yet married."

[35] The angel replied, "God's special power and creative work will make it possible. The Holy Spirit will come upon you, and the power of the Highest Being in Existence will overshadow you. The baby will be supernaturally and miraculously conceived through God's creative work in you. As a result, this sinless baby to be born will be called The Holy One, morally pure and complete in every way. He will be called the Son of God. [36] And listen to this additional detail that will be a sign that all these things are happening: You do not know this yet, but your relative Elizabeth has become pregnant in her old age. People used to talk and gossip about her inability to conceive a child. But she has conceived a son and is now in her sixth month of pregnancy. [37] You see, nothing is impossible with God. No word from God will ever fail because He has the power to make anything happen."

[38] Then Mary responded, "I am the Lord's servant. Even though these things may make others question my marital faithfulness and make me an object of ridicule, I will trust the Lord's goodness and His plan. May everything you have said to me be fulfilled." Then the angel left her.

## 2.2. Defining the Savior's work: Understand that Jesus is the One who fulfills God's plan to make salvation available to all (1:39–80).

### 2.2.1 God has worked throughout human history to make salvation available to everyone through Jesus Christ (1:39–56)

[39] In the days after the angel left, Mary got up and hurried off to the hill country of Judea. She went to the town [40] where Zechariah lived. When she arrived, she entered the house and greeted Elizabeth. [41] When Elizabeth heard Mary's greeting, the baby leaped within her womb. And Elizabeth was filled with the Holy Spirit, which gave her some special insight into the identity of who Mary's baby was and filled her emotions. [42] With a loud, enthusiastic voice, Elizabeth exclaimed to Mary, "God has shown you special favor from among all women, for you will be the mother to a unique child. And God has divinely favored your special child! [43] As I stand here, I am humbled by this moment. I wonder why God would choose to grant me the divine favor and joy of having the mother of my Lord come to visit me? What an incredible privilege! And what an amazing thing that happened the moment you arrived. [44] As soon as the sound of your greeting reached my ears, the baby in my womb jumped for joy! [45] How divinely favored and joyful is the woman who has believed what the Lord said, who believed that He would fulfill His promises to her!"

[46] Mary replied:

> "My soul magnifies the greatness of the Lord, [47] and my spirit rejoices greatly in God my Savior!
> [48] God has looked upon the humble status and lowly situation of His servant girl and changed everything.
> How astonishing is it that God would take His humble servant girl and give her the privilege of serving Him in such a special way! What a privilege to be a model of humble faithfulness that, from now on, will serve all generations by being an example of what it is like to experience God's grace and mercy!
> [49] The Mighty One has done great things for me. But more

importantly, He is holy, having a moral and personal character that is unlike any other.

⁵⁰And His grace and favor are not limited to just me. Regardless of a person's ethnic background or social status, God shows mercy and kindness to any God-fearing person, meaning anyone so devoted to Him that they fear harming His reputation. There is no time limit on God's mercy. From generation to generation, He shows mercy to all the God-fearing people who live for Him.

⁵¹Throughout history, the Lord has done amazing things through the mighty power of His arm. For those not living for Him, He has disrupted and scattered those who are inwardly proud in their thoughts and in the plans and designs of their hearts.

⁵²For rulers who think they are all-powerful and behave arrogantly in their positions, God has knocked them off their thrones and brought them down. But He has also done the reverse: He has lifted up those with a humble attitude.

⁵³He has filled and satisfied the hungry with good things. Yet He has also done the opposite: He has sent the rich, who think they can buy their way to satisfaction, away with empty hands.

⁵⁴Throughout history, the Lord has helped His servant Israel in so many ways; He has always remembered to be merciful to His people.

⁵⁵God has honored the promise He made to our spiritual forefathers, to Abraham and his descendants, that He would continue to show the people who follow Him mercy forever!"

⁵⁶Mary stayed with Elizabeth for about three months (until the birth of John). Then, Mary went back to her home.

> 2.2.2 *God has worked throughout human history to make salvation available to all, and John the Baptist is a prophet who will prepare people for the arrival of God's salvation through Christ (1:57–80).*

⁵⁷When the time came for Elizabeth to have her baby, she gave birth to a son. ⁵⁸When her neighbors and relatives heard that the Lord had shown her great mercy, they celebrated with her.

⁵⁹When the child was eight days old, it was a religious custom to circumcise and name the child. It was also a social custom for the child to receive a name honoring someone in their family. During the circumcision ceremony, those people involved suggested they name the child Zechariah to honor his silent, mute father. ⁶⁰But Elizabeth intervened and said, "No! The child is to be called John."

⁶¹Since that naming was against typical social custom, those involved in the ceremony responded, "Why would you want to name him John? There is no one in among your family or relatives with that name."

⁶²Believing an error was about to be made, they made signs to his father, Zechariah, asking him what he wanted the child to be named. ⁶³Zechariah asked for a writing tablet. On it, Zechariah wrote, "His name is to be John." Everyone was surprised and shocked by his reply. ⁶⁴Immediately after writing that his son's name would be John, Zechariah's silence was broken. His tongue was loosed, and his mouth was able to talk clearly once again. He began speaking and praising God. ⁶⁵A sense of awe and reverential fear came on their entire neighborhood. The news of what had happened spread throughout the hill country of Judea until everyone was talking about had happened. ⁶⁶Everyone who heard about it had the same reaction. They wondered, "The hand of God is clearly upon this child. What special things will this child end up doing?"

⁶⁷Then, the child's father, Zechariah, was filled with the Holy Spirit and prophesied:

> ⁶⁸"Let us praise the Lord, the God of Israel, because He has come to His people and redeemed them by winning a spiritual battle.
> ⁶⁹Like the great strength associated with horned animals but infinitely greater, the Lord has raised up a mighty horn of salvation. He has raised up this mighty horn of salvation for us from the royal lineage of David.
> ⁷⁰God has raised up this mighty Savior precisely as He promised He would through the prophets set apart to serve Him from long ago.

⁷¹He has brought His deliverance to us and saved us from our enemies, from the hands of all who hate us.
⁷²He has shown His mercy and kindness to our spiritual ancestors by remembering and carrying out His holy covenant promise to them, ⁷³fulfilling the oath He swore to our spiritual father Abraham.
⁷⁴By fulfilling His oath and promise, He has rescued us from the hand of our enemies so that we can serve Him without fear, ⁷⁵living divinely consecrated lives before Him that are fully dedicated to following His eternal principles all the days of our lives.

⁷⁶And you, my little child, will be called the prophet of the Highest Being in Existence because you will go before Him to prepare people for His arrival.
⁷⁷You will give His people the knowledge of how to find and receive His salvation through the forgiveness of their sins.
⁷⁸Because of His good, affectionate, and loving mercy, God will bring a saving Sunrise—a supernatural, spiritual morning light—upon us that will change our world forever.
⁷⁹His supernatural light will shine on those living in spiritual darkness and sitting inside the shadow of a spiritually lifeless existence. His saving light will illuminate our way in the world and guide our feet into the path of peace."

⁸⁰As John grew up from childhood to adulthood, he was healthy and became strong in spirit. As an adult, he lived in the isolation of the desert wilderness until the day he began his public, prophetic ministry in Israel.

### 2.3. Celebrating the Savior's arrival: The Savior is born, and heaven celebrates the peace He will bring to the earth (2:1–21).

## CHAPTER 2

¹In those days, Caesar Augustus issued a decree that a census should be taken of the entire Roman Empire. ²It was the first census taken when Quirinius was governor of Syria. ³For the census, everyone had to travel to their ancestral hometown to be registered.

⁴Since Joseph was a descendant of and in the family lineage of David, he needed to return to the city of David, which is called Bethlehem. So Joseph left Nazareth in Galilee and went up to Bethlehem, which was in Judea. ⁵Joseph traveled there with Mary, who was pledged to be married to him and was expecting a child at any moment. ⁶While they were in Bethlehem, the time came for her baby to be born. ⁷She gave birth to her first child, a son. She wrapped him in a cloth blanket and laid him in a manger, because there was no guest lodging or room for them anywhere else.

⁸Later that night, shepherds were staying in the fields nearby. They were keeping a watch over and guarding their flocks of sheep. ⁹As they watched over their flocks, an angel appeared to them, and the blazing brightness of God's glory shone all around them. The angel's presence was so overwhelming that it filled them with fear. ¹⁰Realizing their fear, the angel said to them, "Do not be afraid. I am here to bring you good news that will bring great joy to all people. ¹¹Today, for your benefit, in the city of David, the Savior of the entire world has been born. He is the Christ, the divinely anointed Messiah who will decisively deliver God's people; He is Christ the Lord, the One who has all power and authority and rules over all things. ¹²So that you may know what I am saying is true, I will give you a sign to verify what has been said. When you go into the town of Bethlehem, you will find a baby wrapped in a cloth blanket lying in a manger."

¹³Suddenly, the angel was joined by a vast multitude of angels from the armies of heaven. They formed a vast, angelic choir singing God's praises:

> ¹⁴"God is so worthy of being valued and honored that His worth will always be an infinity of steps beyond what our praise of Him can convey or produce. On earth, the people who know and have responded to His gracious favor will know His peace."

¹⁵When the angels withdrew from sight and returned to the unseen heavenly realm, the shepherds said to one another, "Let us get to Bethlehem as fast as we can and see this amazing thing that has

happened, which the Lord has revealed to us!"

¹⁶They quickly hurried off to town and found Mary, Joseph, and the baby lying in the manger, just as they had been told. ¹⁷After they had seen him, they told everyone what had happened and what the angels had told them about this child. ¹⁸All who heard it marveled at what the shepherds said. ¹⁹But Mary kept all these things stored inside her heart and pondered their significance. ²⁰Then, the shepherds left and returned to their flocks, glorifying and praising God for all the things they had just heard and seen, all the things that had happened exactly as they had been told.

²¹As the eighth day arrived, it was customary to circumcise and name the child. On this day, they named the child Jesus, which was the name the angel had given Him before He was even conceived.

### 2.4. Discovering the Savior: The newborn Savior of the world is recognized as the One who fulfills God's work of salvation throughout history (2:22–40)

²²After the birth of Jesus, His parents participated in three separate ceremonies that were prescribed in the Law of Moses. First, forty days after the birth of a male child, the mother who delivered the child and the child were required to go through a purification ceremony. When the time came for this purification ceremony, Joseph and Mary took the child with them to Jerusalem. At the conclusion of this purification time, they also participated in a second ceremony—the presentation of the firstborn to the Lord, during which they gave their child over to God. ²³(They also participated in a third ceremony—the dedication of firstborn males into the service of the Lord. This third ceremony was performed as commanded in the Law of Lord in Exodus 13 that says, "Every firstborn male child must be set apart and consecrated to the Lord.") ²⁴As part of the first ceremony—the purification ceremony—those involved in the child's birth offered a burnt sacrifice and sin offering to be purified from any uncleanness picked up during the delivery. Those who could afford it offered a lamb as a sacrifice; those who were poor and could not afford it offered a pigeon. Mary and Joseph offered two pigeons. This rite fulfilled what is said in the Law

of the Lord in Leviticus 12:8: "a pair of turtledoves and two young pigeons."

²⁵Now, while Mary and Joseph were in Jerusalem for these required ceremonies, there was a man there named Simeon. He was a devout man who lived according to God's teachings. Simeon was eagerly looking forward to and anticipating the day when God would fulfill His promise to rescue Israel through the coming of the Messiah. The Holy Spirit was upon Simeon, ²⁶and He had revealed to Simeon that he would not die before he had seen the Lord's Messiah, the Anointed and Appointed One who would decisively deliver God's people.

²⁷Led by the Spirit, Simeon went to the Temple courts. On that very day, Mary and Joseph also came to the Temple courts to present and dedicate their baby, Jesus, to the Lord as God's law required. ²⁸When Simeon was allowed to take the child into his arms, he praised God, saying,

> ²⁹"Sovereign Lord who orders all existence for Your purposes, You have fulfilled Your promise to me and allowed me to see Your Christ, Your Anointed One who will deliver your people. Having fulfilled Your call on my life, Your servant can now depart in peace.
> ³⁰My eyes have seen Your salvation, ³¹which You have prepared for all people and put on full public display for all nations to know.
> ³²He is a light that reveals God to all the non-Jewish nations; He is the highest expression of Your value and worth and Your promises fulfilled through Israel."

³³Jesus' father and mother marveled at what was being said about Him. ³⁴Then Simeon asked God to continue to show His favor to Jesus' parents. He said to His mother, Mary, "Listen carefully to what I am about to share with you. This child is destined to cause the rise and fall of many people in Israel. He has been sent as a sign from God, but He will split the nation in two, and many will oppose Him. ³⁵As people encounter Jesus, their true hearts will be revealed. And you, Mary, will not be immune from pain either. Seeing His rejection will hurt you as though a sword has pierced your side and your very soul."

³⁶While they were at the Temple, there was also a prophetess there named Anna, the daughter of Penuel from the tribe of Asher. She was very old. After being married seven years, her husband died. ³⁷Since that time, she had lived as a widow for a long time and now was eighty-four years old. Her devotion to God was strong; she never left the Temple area. She stayed there day and night, worshipping, fasting, and praying to God. ³⁸She approached Mary and Joseph the very moment Simeon was finishing his prayer of blessing on them. She began praising and thanking God for their child. She talked about their child, Jesus, to all who had been eagerly anticipating Jerusalem's redemption, liberation, and deliverance.

³⁹When Joseph and Mary had performed all the rituals and rites the Law of Moses required, they left for Galilee and returned to their hometown of Nazareth. ⁴⁰The child Jesus grew up healthy, strong, and full of wisdom. God's grace and favor were upon Him.

### 2.5. Discovering the Savior: The Savior of the world is fully human but knows, throughout His life, that He is serving and fulfilling God's plan of salvation (2:41–52).

⁴¹As was custom for all Jewish people, Jesus' parents traveled annually to Jerusalem for the Festival of the Passover, which celebrated Israel's freedom from Egypt during the Exodus. ⁴²When Jesus was twelve years old, His family made the annual journey to Jerusalem as usual. ⁴³After the festival celebration was over, the traveling caravan of Joseph's and Mary's relatives and friends left to return to Nazareth. However, unknown to His parents, the boy Jesus stayed behind in Jerusalem. ⁴⁴Jesus' parents assumed He was a part of the large traveling caravan, and they had traveled for an entire day before they began looking for Him among their group of relatives and friends. ⁴⁵When they failed to find Him, they made the day's journey back to Jerusalem to look for Him.

⁴⁶After three days, they found Jesus in the Temple courts. He was sitting among the religious teachers, listening to them and asking questions. ⁴⁷Everyone who heard the boy Jesus was amazed at His

level of learning and the depth of insight in the answers He was giving. ⁴⁸However, when Jesus' parents found Him, they were practically overwhelmed with gladness but also familial frustration. His mother said to Him, "Son, why have You done this to us and scared us half to death? Your father and I have been deeply distressed as we have been frantically and anxiously searching for you everywhere."

⁴⁹Jesus replied, "Why were you searching for Me? Did you not know that I must be in My Father's house, focused on My Father's way?" ⁵⁰But Jesus' parents did not understand what He was saying to them or what He meant by it.

⁵¹The boy Jesus left Jerusalem with His parents, and they all went down to Nazareth. He lived there obediently with them. His mother did not understand everything about these childhood events, but she kept them and pondered them in her heart. ⁵²Throughout adolescence and adulthood, Jesus grew in wisdom and stature and in favor with God and all people.

**3.** Clarifying God's plan of salvation: Jesus demonstrates that He is qualified to represent both humanity and God's people as the Messiah, the One who will bring salvation (3:1–4:13).

   **3.1.** John the Baptist makes it clear: One must decide to follow Jesus and make a clear, conscious commitment to following Him or suffer the consequences before God (3:1-20).

### CHAPTER 3

¹Fifteen years into Tiberius Caesar's reign over the Roman Empire, Rome ruled the social and political world. During this time, Pontius Pilate served Rome as governor over all Judea; Herod Antipas was another class of Roman provincial official who ruled over the region of Galilee, providing an appearance of Jewish self-government on Rome's behalf; Herod's brother Philip was a Roman provincial official who ruled over the regions of Iturea and Traconitis; and Lysanias was a Roman provincial official who ruled over the region of Abilene.

²During this time, the former Jewish high priest Annas and those associated with his family dominated the religious landscape of Israel. Unofficially, the retired Annas continued to be very influential while serving as an honorary high priest. Officially, it was Caiaphas, Annas's son-in-law, who served as the high priest. Into this social, political, and religious landscape, the word of God came to John, Zechariah's son, while he was living in the wilderness.

³After receiving this message, John went into all the region around the Jordan River preaching a baptism of repentance, which symbolized a person's definitive change of mind by turning away from things that would lead them away from God and turning to Him to receive forgiveness and follow His way. Unlike the repeated baptisms Jewish people knew related to ritual cleansing, the baptism John preached was a one-time baptism signifying that one had turned their entire being—heart and mind—to God and was ready for the arrival of God's salvation.

⁴In the Scriptures of the Old Covenant in Isaiah 40:3-5, the prophet Isaiah spoke of John and described the purpose of his ministry:

> "A voice will speak with powerful and moving force calling out to everyone from the deserted wilderness, saying, 'Prepare the way for the Lord's arrival!'
> "Make the path for His arrival smooth and straight!
> ⁵Every valley shall be filled; every mountain and hill shall be leveled.
> The curvy roads shall be straightened; the rough roads shall be made smooth.
> ⁶And then, with the seemingly immovable now removed, all people will be ready to see God's salvation."

⁷When the crowds came out to the wilderness to hear John, he said to them, "You all are like a group of snakes trying to flee a fire! You all sense that God's fire of judgment is coming. But do you really think you can slither down here to the river, dip your toes in the water, and escape His judgment? ⁸If you understand this message and turn your entire being—your hearts and your minds—to God, then prove it by the way you live. If you have turned to God, then that inward reality,

like a tree, should produce outward fruit in your life. It is not enough to claim your cultural, religious, or family heritage, saying, 'We have Abraham as our spiritual forefather and are of his lineage.' That heritage does not reflect your individual choice; it will not save you. After all, if God just wants heartless, mindless followers, He can create those from these stones if He desires. ⁹What matters is an individual's entire being—heart and mind—turned to God and producing outward fruit. And this is an urgent matter. Even now, the axe of God's judgment rests near the root of the trees. Every tree that does not produce good, outward fruit that reflects a genuine, inward faith will be cut down and thrown into the fire."

¹⁰ The crowds responded, "What kind of actions can we do to demonstrate that we are producing fruit?"

¹¹John replied, "If you have two coats, you should give one to the person who does not have one. If you have plenty of food, you should share it with those who are going hungry."

¹²Tax collectors—who were typically known to abuse people by taking too much commission when collecting taxes—came to be baptized as a symbol of their life change toward God. They were also eager to know what to do and asked, "Teacher, what kind of actions demonstrate that we, as tax collectors, are producing fruit?"

¹³John responded, "Do not extort people by taking inflated commissions any longer. When you collect taxes, only collect the taxes that are required and take a normal and appropriate commission as would be expected."

¹⁴Baptized soldiers were also curious. They asked, "What kind of actions demonstrate that we, as soldiers, are producing fruit?"

John replied to them, "Do not use your position to extort money by terrifying others with your power or bringing false accusations against people to blackmail money from them. Be content with your pay and do not abuse your position and power.

¹⁵During this time, all of these God-fearing people were eagerly waiting

for God's Anointed One to come, for the arrival of His Messiah that would decisively deliver His people. In their eagerness, they began to wonder if John might actually by the Messiah.

[16]John answered them all by saying, "I am baptizing you with an outward symbol of water. It is merely an outward symbol of the inward reality you claim. However, there is One coming who is far greater, far superior than I am. He is so much greater than I that I am not even worthy to serve as His slave, not even worthy of performing the smallest of tasks for Him, such as loosening the straps of His sandals. His baptism is infinitely more substantial. He will baptize you with the Holy Spirit's presence and with a purging fire that burns inside you. [17]And do not think this is something you can put off. The harvest is imminent. His winnowing fork is in His hand, and He is ready to clear the threshing floor. When His winnowing fork lifts the grain into the air, it will gather the intended wheat into His barn, but it will also separate out the undesired chaff, which will be burned with a never-ending fire." [18]With many other teachings and words of warning, John proclaimed God's good news of repentance and deliverance to all the people.

[19]John also publicly rebuked Herod Antipas, the Roman provincial official who ruled over Galilee, for his scandalous marriage to Herodias (who was his brother's wife) and for all the other evils things he had done. [20]The result: Herod added on to his many other evils by having John the Baptist put in prison.

### 3.2. God makes it clear: Jesus is God's Son who will reveal His truth and salvation to the world (3:21–22).

[21]One day before John was imprisoned, when many other people were being baptized, Jesus was also baptized. As Jesus was praying, the unseen, spiritual realm of heaven opened up [22]and the Holy Spirit descended on Him in a visible, spiritual form that looked like a dove. Then a voice from heaven said, "You are My deeply loved Son who is the Sovereign King over all things. I have chosen You and marked You with My love. With Your power, presence, and ability to reveal the truth to the world, I find overwhelming joy!"

## 3.3. The history of God's work makes it clear: Jesus fulfills God's promises to His people and is the One who brings salvation to all (3:23–38).

²³When Jesus began His public ministry, He was about thirty years old. But His roots and qualifications for being the Messiah were far deeper. Since tracing the ancestry of the Messiah is an integral part of Jewish thinking—tracing the Messiah's roots back to David, Abraham, and Adam—let us look at Jesus's genealogy and see how He is qualified to be the Messiah. Let us see how Jesus is the last and vital link in God fulfilling His promises to His people throughout history.

> Even though Jesus was born of the Virgin Mary, Jesus was known as the legal son of Joseph.
> Joseph was the son of Heli.
> ²⁴Heli was the son of Matthat.
> Matthat was the son of Levi.
> Levi was the son of Melki.
> Melki was the son of Jannai.
> Jannai was the son of Joseph.
> ²⁵Joseph was the son of Mattathias.
> Mattathias was the son of Amos.
> Amos was the son of Nahum.
> Nahum was the son of Esli
> Esli was the son of Naggai.
> ²⁶Naggai was the son of Maath.
> Maath was the son of Mattathias.
> Mattathias was the son of Semein.
> Semein was the son of Josech.
> Josech was the son of Joda.
> ²⁷Joda was the son of Jonan.
> Jonan was the son of Rhesa.
> Rhesa was the son of Zerubbel.
> Zerubbel was the son of Shealtiel.
> Shealtiel was the son of Neri.
> ²⁸Neri was the son of Melki.
> Melki was the son of Addi.
> Addi was the son of Cosam.
> Cosam was the son of Elmadam.

Elmadam was the son of Er.
²⁹Er was the son of Joshua.
Joshua was the son of Eliezer.
Eliezer was the son of Jorim.
Jorim was the son of Matthat.
Matthat was the son of Levi.
³⁰Levi was the son of Simeon.
Simeon was the son of Judah.
Judah was the son of Joseph.
Joseph was the son of Jonam.
Jonam was the son of Eliakim.
³¹Eliakim was the son of Melea.
Melea was the son of Menna.
Menna was the son of Mattatha.
Mattatha was the son of Nathan.
Nathan was the son of David.

³²David was the son of Jesse.
Jesse was the son of Obed.
Obed was the son of Boaz.
Boaz was the son of Salmon.
Salmon was the son of Nashon.
³³Nashon was the son of Amminiadab.
Amminiadab was the son of Admin.
Admin was the son of Arni.
Arni was the son of Hezron.
Hezron was the son of Perez.
Perez was the son of Judah.
³⁴Judah was the son of Jacob.
Jacob was the son of Isaac.
Isaac was the son of Abraham.

Abraham was the son of Terah.
Terah was the son of Nahor.
³⁵Nahor was the son of Serug.
Serug was the son of Reu.
Reu was the son of Peleg.
Peleg was the son of Eber.
Eber was the son of Shelah.

³⁶Shelah was the son of Cainan.
Cainan was the son of Arphaxad.
Arphaxad was the son of Shem.
Shem was the son of Noah.
Noah was the son of Lamech.
³⁷Lamech was the son of Methuselah.
Methuselah was the son of Enoch.
Enoch was the son of Jared.
Jared was the son of Mahalalel.
Mahalalel was the son of Kenan.
³⁸Kenan was the son of Enosh.
Enosh was the son of Seth
Seth was the son of Adam.
Adam was the son of God.

**3.4. Jesus' actions make it clear: Jesus resists the devil's temptation and does not deviate from God's plan to make salvation available to all (4:1–13).**

## CHAPTER 4

¹Jesus, full of the Holy Spirit, returned from the Jordan River valley. However, before beginning His public ministry, the Spirit led Him into the deserted wilderness ²where He was tempted by the devil for forty days. During those days, Jesus ate nothing and was very hungry.

³The devil appeared to Him and appealed to His hunger, using it as a means of tempting Jesus to question God's provision and care. The devil said to Him, "If You are the Son of God, then why are You starving? Do You not have the power to tell these stones to become bread?"

⁴Jesus did not give in to the temptation to act independently and rebelliously against the Father and His will. Jesus replied, "To follow God is to live, and I shall live according to God's will. I will follow what is written in Deuteronomy 8:3, which says, 'Life is defined by more than what you eat or consume.'"

⁵Then the devil took Jesus up to a high place and showed Him all the kingdoms of the world at one time. ⁶Attempting to get Jesus to abandon His loyalty to the Father and bypass the long path of obedience

that lay ahead, the devil said to Him, "Do You want the world to follow You? I will give You all the authority, power, worship, and adoration of all the people, nations, and kingdoms of the world. I am the ruler of this domain, and these nations and kingdoms belong to me. I can give them to anyone I want. ⁷If You will worship me and follow me, I will give it all to You."

⁸Jesus resisted this temptation by replying, "I shall live according to God's will and remain loyal to serving Him. I will follow what is written in Deuteronomy 6:13, which says, 'Worship the Lord your God and serve only Him.'"

⁹Then, the devil took Jesus to Jerusalem and had Him stand on the highest point of the Temple. Attempting to challenge His trust in God's protection and care, the devil said to Him, "If You are really the Son of God, then jump off. Would that not demonstrate and enhance Your dependence on God's care? ¹⁰ After all, for those who live according to God's will, it says in Psalm 91:11-12,

> "God will direct His angels in regards to You,
> To carefully guard and protect You.
> ¹¹They will catch You if You fall;
> They will make sure You do not even stub Your toe on a stone."

¹²Jesus resisted this temptation by replying, "You fail to represent the Scripture's teaching faithfully. You are proposing a presumptuous testing of God's care that would demonstrate a lack of faith in Him. I shall live according to God's will and follow what is written in Deuteronomy 6:16, which says, 'Do not test the Lord your God.'"

¹³When the devil had finished tempting Jesus with no success, he left Him and resolved to wait for another window of opportunity to come.

4. Recognizing the Savior: Will people recognize who Jesus is? [The Galilean Ministry] (4:14–9:50).

## 4.1. Jesus demonstrates who He is through His powerful teaching and actions (4: 14–44).

### 4.1.1. Jesus' teaching conveys the divine truth He came to reveal to the world (4:14–30).

[14] After the period of temptation had ended, Jesus returned to Galilee full of the Holy Spirit's power. Because of His words and actions, news about Jesus spread quickly through the entire region. [15] As He taught in the synagogues, everyone was impressed with Jesus and praised Him for His teaching. [16] While Jesus was traveling through the area and teaching others, one day He came to Nazareth, His boyhood home. As was His custom, Jesus went to the synagogue on the Sabbath.

The typical Jewish synagogue service started with reciting the Shema (Deuteronomy 6:4-9), followed by a time of prayer. Then there would be a reading of the Old Covenant Scriptures from both the Mosaic Law (the first five books in the Old Covenant) and another from a passage in the Prophets. An exposition (or teaching) would follow that tied the readings together.

When the time in the service came to hear God's Word, Jesus stood up to read the Scriptures. [17] He was handed the scroll of the prophet Isaiah. He unrolled the scroll to Isaiah 61:1-2 and read it, mixing in an allusion to Isaiah 58:6. Jesus read the following:

> [18] "The Spirit of the Lord is upon Me,
>   because He has appointed and anointed Me
>   to announce God's message of good news to the poor.
> He has sent Me to proclaim that those living in debt of all kinds—
>   materially, socially, and economically but, most importantly,
>   those living in spiritual debt—will be set free;
> that those living in blindness of all kinds—physically, but most
>   importantly, those living in spiritual blindness—will recover
>   their sight;
> that those living in oppression of all kinds—physically, but most
>   importantly, those living under spiritual bondage—will be
>   set free; [19] and

to announce that the appointed and accepted time of the Lord's deliverance, of His salvation, has come."

[20]Following the customary service order, Jesus rolled up the scroll, handed it back to the attendant, and sat down to teach. Because the passage Jesus read referenced God's deliverance, combined with the intrigue of wondering who Jesus was, everyone was eager to hear what His teaching would be on this text. [21]Jesus began by saying to them, "Today, this Scripture from Isaiah has been fulfilled in your presence; the new era of God's salvation has arrived!"

[22]Everyone was impressed by what He said and how He said it. More importantly, they were amazed at His proclamation of God's grace and that He claimed to be fulfilling God's promise of salvation. Yet they were skeptical and could not help but question what Jesus said. They asked, "How can this guy be God's Anointed Prophet, the Messiah who will bring deliverance to God's people? Is He not Joseph's son? He cannot be the Messiah; His standing in society is not right."

[23]Then Jesus said to them, "Undoubtedly, you will quote this proverb to Me: 'If you are such a great doctor, then heal yourself.' And you will tell Me, 'We have heard of You doing many great things in Capernaum. So, now, show us some of Your mighty power and miracles here in Your hometown, and then we will believe You.'

[24]"But I am telling you this truth: No prophet is accepted in his hometown. It would not matter what mighty work I performed before you; you would still have your doubts. [25]The truth of the situation is that we are in one of the least spiritual periods of our history, much like it was in the days of the prophets Elijah and Elisha, and no matter what I did, you would have your doubts. But regardless of your response and belief, God will bring His deliverance to those who do believe. For example, in the days of Elijah, there were three and a half years of drought and famine throughout the land. It produced a large number of needy widows who needed much help in Israel. [26]Yet their trust in the Lord and receptivity to Him was so low that God did not send Elijah to any of these Israelites. Instead, God sent Elijah to a Gentile foreigner who demonstrated more faith—the non-Jewish widow from Zarephath who lived in the Gentile region of Sidon. [27]During the time

of the prophet Elisha, there were many Israelites with leprosy. Yet their propensity to receive any spiritual truth was so low that God did not send Elisha to heal any of the Israelite lepers. Instead, God sent Elisha only to heal the non-Jewish leper Naaman, who was from Syria, a Gentile country."

[28]When the people in the Jewish synagogue heard Jesus' clear assessment of their spiritual state and condition, they were furious and filled with rage. [29]A mob of people rose up and drove Him out of the town. They were so mad they took Him to a cliff on which the town was built with the intent of throwing Him off the cliff to His death. [30]But Jesus was able to maneuver away from the crowd and then went on His way.

> 4.1.2 Jesus' actions reflect the divine compassion He came to reveal to the world (4:31–44).

[31]After leaving Nazareth, Jesus went down to Capernaum, a prominent Jewish center of trade in the region. While there, as was His custom, Jesus taught in the synagogue on the Sabbath. [32]The people there were overwhelmed and amazed at His teaching. Unlike other teachers who made their point by referring back to what God had done in the past or how their words were in line with other accepted teachings, Jesus taught differently. When Jesus taught, He did not speak with derived authority like others. Instead, Jesus declared God's will directly and with complete power and authority.

[33]One day, while teaching at the synagogue, a man possessed by an unclean spirit of evil began shouting out loud to Jesus, saying, [34]"What are You doing here? Get out of here; go away! Why do You want to interfere with and bother us, Jesus of Nazareth? Have You come to destroy us? After all, we know Your identity and who You are—the Holy One of God!"

[35]The demon attempted to overpower Jesus' authority by calling out His name, but it did not work. Jesus, being more powerful, rebuked the demon and said, "Be quiet and stop your talking! Come out of this man right now!" At Jesus' word, the demon threw the man down to the ground in an attempt to hurt the man, and then the demon came out of the man. The demon's attempt to hurt the man had failed, as

the man was without injury.

³⁶The people were speechless and amazed. They said to one another, "What kind of teaching is this? His words are filled with so much power and authority that even evil spirits come out at His command! What kind of incredible teaching is this where such powerful words and deeds work together for one's deliverance?" ³⁷The people were so enthralled with what Jesus was saying and doing that the news about Him spread through every town in the region.

³⁸When Jesus left the synagogue that day, He went to Simon's home. Simon's mother-in-law was suffering from a very high fever. As was custom of these days, fevers were viewed as a form of divine judgment and only curable by divine intervention. The people of Simon's home asked Jesus to help Simon's mother-in-law. ³⁹Standing by her bedside, Jesus rebuked the fever. When He did, the fever left her. She immediately got up, and her recovery from Jesus' healing was so full and complete that she began to prepare dinner for them.

⁴⁰As the sun was setting that evening, people brought to Jesus all those who were sick from various diseases. He laid hands on every one of them, and they were healed. ⁴¹Many demon-possessed people also approached Jesus. They tried to trouble Him or gain power over Him by calling out His name, shouting, "We know who You are; You are the Son of God!" But their attempts never worked. Jesus rebuked them and would not allow them to speak anymore, because He did not want their demonic confession of Him to be circulating publicly.

⁴²Very early the next morning, while it was still dark and daylight was just starting to break, Jesus went out to an isolated and solitary place. The crowds of people were searching for Him everywhere. When they finally found Him, they tried to prevent Jesus from leaving the area. ⁴³However, Jesus responded to them by reinforcing His mission and purpose among them. He said, "I must move on to other towns so that I can publicly proclaim the good news of God's kingdom there as well. I have been sent to this world for this purpose—to proclaim the good news of God's kingdom as the place of ultimate freedom, deliverance, and salvation, where the forces of evil are overcome." ⁴⁴So Jesus continued preaching in the synagogues throughout Judea.

**4.2. Jesus introduces a new era with a new way of God working in the world, one that will transform lives and encounters opposition to God's plan (5:1–6:16).**

*4.2.1. Jesus transforms lives as He calls people to follow Him and demonstrates His power to change people's lives (5:1–32).*

## CHAPTER 5

*4.2.1.a. Jesus calls ordinary, everyday people to be His disciples (5:1-11).*

¹One day, as Jesus was proclaiming God's message to a large crowd by the Lake of Gennesaret (also known as the Sea of Galilee), the large crowd pressed in on Him very tightly to listen to God's Word. ²Standing by the lake, Jesus noticed two empty boats tied up at the water's edge. The fishermen had just stepped off them and were washing their nets. ³Jesus stepped into one of the boats, the one that was owned by Simon. He asked Simon to push the boat out a little from the shore. Then, from the boat, Jesus was able to sit down and teach the large crowd on the shore from a more effective position.

⁴When Jesus had finished speaking, He asked Simon, "While we are out on the water, how about pushing out into the deep water and letting your nets down for a nice catch of fish?"

⁵Simon answered, "Master Teacher, we are professional fishermen and worked hard all night and did not catch anything. These current conditions are less than ideal for fishing. But, if You say so, then I will go back out and let the nets down again."

⁶When they let the nets down, they caught such a large number of fish that their nets were about to break from the weight. ⁷They shouted to their partners in the other boat to come and help them with the catch. The result: the yield of fish was so great that it filled both boats, and both boats were so full of fish that they were almost on the verge of sinking.

⁸When Simon Peter saw all this, he realized something miraculous had happened—something only an agent of God could have done. In humility, Simon Peter fell to his knees and said, "Lord, You should leave me. I am too much of a sinner for You to be around me." ⁹Peter was astonished at the catch of fish and in fearful awe of Jesus' power and who He must be. But Peter was not alone. The others there with him had the same reaction. ¹⁰Simon's fishing partners, James and John, the sons of Zebedee, were also astonished and fearfully amazed by Jesus.

Then Jesus replied to Simon's awestruck humility: "Do not be afraid; there is nothing to fear. What you have seen here is just a hint of the greater things to come. I invite you to follow Me. From now on, in your new work and service, you will be fishing for people and leading them to learn a new way of life." ¹¹When the boat landed back on shore, they left everything and followed Jesus.

> 4.2.1.b.  Jesus touches those who others consider untouchable: the healing of the leper (5:12-16).

¹²While Jesus was traveling through one town, a man covered with leprosy approached Him. When the man with leprosy—a man who had long been ostracized from society as a social outcast and who had not experienced a physical touch in years—saw Jesus, he fell facedown before Him. He begged Jesus, "Lord, I am confident that You have the capacity and ability to heal disease. If You are willing, You can heal my leprosy and make me clean."

¹³Jesus responded by reaching out His hand and touching the man, and said, "I am willing. You are now healed!" At Jesus' word, immediately, the leprosy disappeared.

¹⁴Then Jesus gave him further instructions, "Do not tell anyone what happened here. Instead, follow the legal requirements of Moses' command in Leviticus 14. Go show yourself to the priest and take the offering required for your cleansing. It will be a testimony of proof to them about your transformation, and it will help them understand that you have been cleansed."

¹⁵Despite these instructions, the news of the healing was too combustible to keep quiet—the story about what had happened spread quickly. As a result, large crowds came to listen to Jesus' teaching and to be healed of their diseases. ¹⁶Yet, even though He was now attracting larger crowds, Jesus often withdrew to isolated, deserted spots in the wilderness for times of prayer.

> 4.2.1.c. Jesus visually demonstrates how His power can heal through faith in Him: the healing of people with paralysis (5:17-26).

¹⁷One day while Jesus was teaching, some Pharisees and teachers of the Jewish religious law were sitting among the crowd gathered around Him. People had come from nearly every village of Galilee and from Judea and Jerusalem. The power of the Lord to heal was strong with Jesus. ¹⁸A group of men came to where Jesus was and were carrying a paralyzed man lying on a mat. They were looking for a way to get inside the house so they could set the paralyzed man in front of Jesus. ¹⁹However, they could not find a way to maneuver through the vast crowd to achieve their goal. Not giving up, they went up onto the flat, sloping roof of the house. They dug through the reeds, branches, and dried mud that composed the roof—creating an opening through it—and lowered the paralyzed man on his mat down through the roof, placing him right in front of Jesus.

²⁰When Jesus saw the visible outworking of their faith, He said to the paralyzed man, "Friend, your sins are forgiven."

²¹These words ignited outrage in the Pharisees and teachers of the Jewish religious law. They began saying to themselves, "Who does this guy think He is? Only God alone has the power and authority to forgive sins. What this guy is saying is a blasphemous insult to God!"

²²Jesus knew what they were thinking. He asked them, "Why do you doubt and question My power and abilities in your hearts? ²³Which do you think is easier: 1) to speak a theological declaration to the paralyzed man saying, 'Your sins are forgiven,' or 2) to provide empirical proof that his sins are forgiven by saying, 'Stand up and walk'? ²⁴So that you may know the Son of Man has authority on earth to forgive sins, I will show you." Then Jesus turned to the paralytic man and said,

"Stand up, pick up your mat, and go to your home."

²⁵Immediately, the man stood up in front of them, picked up the mat he had been lying on, and went away to his home, praising God the entire way. ²⁶Everyone who witnessed this act was overwhelmed and amazed. Full of awe and wonder, they praised God, saying, "We have seen amazing, extraordinary things today!"

> 4.2.1.d. Jesus demonstrates a pattern of reaching out to those on the edge of society: the calling a tax collector (5:27-32).

²⁷Later on, as Jesus left the town, He saw a tax collector named Levi. Levi was sitting at his toll booth, collecting the surcharge tax as people traveled from town to town. Jesus took the initiative with Levi and invited him, saying, "From now on, follow and learn from Me."

²⁸Levi responded. He got up, left everything, and followed Jesus.

²⁹Then Levi held a great party in his house to honor and celebrate Jesus. Levi invited many of the people he knew—other tax collectors and those considered "sinners" by the religious elite. A large crowd of Levi's notorious "sinner" friends was eating and relaxing together with Jesus and His followers at the dinner table. ³⁰But the Pharisees and the teachers of the Jewish religion were bitter about this action. From their perspective, socializing with people communicated acceptance of their values. So, they griped and complained to Jesus' disciples, "Why in the world are you all attending this dinner party and associating yourselves with despicable tax collectors and well-known sinners?"

³¹Jesus answered them, "It is not the healthy who need a doctor, but those who are sick. ³²I have not come to call those who think they are self-sufficient to live a new kind of life before God. Instead, I have come to call those who know they need help to live a new kind of life with God, commanding them to have a change of heart and mind that will ultimately change their entire being."

> 4.2.2. Jesus introduces a new era of God's work and a new way of God working in the world (5:33-6:5).
>
> 4.2.2.a. Jesus introduces a new era of God working in the world

(5:33-39).

³³"Then, the Pharisees and teachers of the Jewish religious law made another inquiry. They said to Jesus, "John the Baptist's disciples fast and offer up prolonged periods of special prayer regularly. To us, these solemn acts are major displays of devotion to, respect for, and worship of God. So why is it that Your disciples spend more time eating, drinking, and having a good time than they do engaging in solemn fasting and devotion?"

³⁴Jesus answered them, "Right now, they are celebrating God's kingdom, which is presently at hand and among us. Their celebration is like being guests of the Groom at His wedding reception. On such a festive occasion, should these guests dishonor the Groom by not eating and joining in the celebration with Him? Of course they should not abstain; they should join in and celebrate with the Groom. ³⁵However, a time is coming when the Groom will be taken away from them. When that time comes, they will need to fast."

³⁶Jesus continued by sharing three illustrations of how the new era of God's kingdom had brought new perspectives with its arrival. Jesus said, "First, no one tears of a piece of cloth from a piece of new, unshrunk fabric and uses it to sew a patch on an old garment. If they do, the new patch will shrink when washed, making the tear in the old garment even worse than it was to begin with. And it will ruin the new cloth too.

³⁷"Second, no one puts new wine into old wine bottles. If one does, the new wine, as it expands during fermentation, will break the old wine bottles because they have become inflexible over time (as the animal skin that they are made from has dried out and become stiff). If one tries to put new wine into old wine bottles, both the new wine and the old bottles would be ruined. ³⁸Instead, it is best to put new wine into new wine bottles that are flexible (as they are made of skin that is not dried out and are shapeable).

³⁹"Third, no one who likes old wine will develop a taste for new wine. They are far too comfortable with their old ways and have already have made up their minds, saying, 'The old wine is just fine and good enough for me.' No matter how good the new wine is, some people

will never change their perspective."

## CHAPTER 6

> 4.2.2.b. Jesus introduces a new way of God working in the world—through the demonstration of the Son of Man's authority (6:1-5).

¹On one particular Sabbath, as Jesus was walking through some grain fields, His disciples began breaking off the heads of the grain, rubbing off the husks in their hands, and eating the grain. ²However, some Pharisees who had been watching them closely said, "Why are you breaking religious laws by harvesting grain on the Sabbath? Do you not know there are specific religious laws about not doing that on the Sabbath?"

³Jesus replied, "Have you ever read the Scriptures? Have you ever read in 1 Samuel 21 and 22 what David and his companions did when they were hungry? ⁴David entered the house of God, the Holy Temple, took consecrated bread right off the altar, and ate it—the very bread that, by specific religious laws, only priests are supposed to eat. And not only did he eat it himself, he also handed it out to his companions as well."

⁵Then Jesus said to them, "If you are going to condemn these disciples, then you must condemn David, the king who is a model of the Messiah who will deliver God's people, as well. But there is a more significant point here that you need to recognize. The Son of Man is the Lord who exercises authority over all things. He has the right to regulate what takes place anywhere and anytime, including what happens on the Sabbath."

> 4.2.3 Jesus encounters opposition to His authority and the new way of God working in the world (6:6-16).

⁶On another Sabbath, as was His custom, Jesus went into the synagogue and was teaching. A man with a shriveled and deformed right hand was also there. ⁷The teachers of the Jewish religious law and the Pharisees were spying on every move Jesus made. They were looking

for a reason to bring formal accusations against Jesus, so they watched the man with the deformed hand to see if Jesus would break a Sabbath law by healing on the Sabbath. ⁸But Jesus knew their intentions and what they were thinking. He said to the man with the deformed right hand, "Come and stand up here in front so that everyone can see you." The man did as Jesus instructed.

⁹Then Jesus posed a question to everyone there, "I have a question for you. What do your religious laws tell us about what we should do on the Sabbath—should we do good or evil? On the Sabbath, should we save life or destroy it?"

¹⁰He glanced around the room, looking each person directly in their eyes, one by one. Then Jesus said to the man, "Stretch out your hand and let us see how God answers that question." When the man stretched out his hand, it was fully restored to complete health. ¹¹But when this happened, the Pharisees and teachers of the Jewish religious law were furious. Concerned about their religious laws and their interpretations about God and His ways, they went outside and began talking with one another about what they should do to stop Jesus.

¹²Around this time, as the Jewish religious opposition was growing stronger against Him, Jesus took a strategic retreat up on a mountain. It was an all-night retreat where He spent the entire time praying to God. ¹³When morning came, Jesus called His disciples together and chose twelve of them to be His apostles, the ones He would entrust with His authority and appoint as His special, authoritative ambassadors to publicly represent His message of God's kingdom to the world. The twelve apostles whom He appointed were: ¹⁴Simon (to whom Jesus gave the name Peter), Andrew (who was Peter's brother), James, John, Philip, Bartholomew, ¹⁵Matthew, Thomas, James (who was the son of Alphaeus), Simon (who was called the Zealot), ¹⁶Judas (who was the son of James), and Judas (who later became Jesus' betrayer).

### 4.3. Jesus teaches a new way, a new pattern of living for God (6:17–49).

¹⁷When Jesus came down from the mountain with His newly appointed apostles, He stood on a large, level plain surrounded by many of His

disciples. They were soon joined by a vast, even larger crowd of people from all over Judea and Jerusalem and the coastal region around Tyre and Sidon. [18]They came from all over for two purposes: to hear Jesus' teaching and to be healed by Him from their diseases. And those troubled by evil, impure spirits were healed. [19]With so much of Jesus' healing power on display, and with so many people healed, everyone tried to touch Him.

> 4.3.1. *Jesus identifies those who are truly fortunate before God and those who are not (6:20-26).*

[20]On this occasion, Jesus turned His attention from the demonstration of His power at work to highlight for His disciples the essential teaching on how His followers should live. He taught them, saying:

"In the economy of God's kingdom, appearances can be deceiving. Those who are truly fortunate before God may not be the ones you might think. Let Me share with you a portrait of those for whom God has compassion.

> "The truly fortunate ones are you who are poor and realize your need for God,
> because you have a position in the kingdom of God.
>
> [21]"The truly fortunate ones before God are you who are hungry and lack the material resources even to meet your hunger,
> because you have God's promise that all your needs will be filled and ultimately satisfied.
>
> "The truly fortunate ones before God are you who weep under the strain of life's struggles and experience pain, strain, or rejection as you live for God,
> because you will be filled with a joy that overflows into laughter.
>
> [22]"The truly fortunate ones before God are you who are suffering hatred, social ostracism and exclusion, insult, and rejection to the point your community considers you a wicked shame because you follow the Son of Man.
> [23]When this happens, you can rejoice and leap for joy because

your reward is great in heaven. And know that you are not alone in the way you are being treated. Your spiritual ancestors, the prophets of the Old Covenant, were treated the same way.

[24]"While some people will be fortunate before God because they seek Him, others will know disaster before Him.

"How disastrous it will be before God for you who are rich and have become spiritually self-sufficient and callous toward others,
because the only comfort and happiness you will have will be in your material wealth that you cannot take with you into eternity.

[25]"How disastrous it will before God for you who have the material resources that allow you to be well-fed and prosperous now,
because a time of deep, lasting, and terrible hunger awaits you.

"How disastrous it will be before God for you who ignore Him and the needs of others to pursue a happy, comfortable, good life now,
because a time is coming when all your good times and so-called happiness will turn into deep, lasting mourning and weeping.

[26]"How disastrous it will be before God for you who are praised by others, whose lives are oriented toward pleasing others instead of living God's way,
because the false prophets of old, who received a terrible eternal fate, were treated with similar public praise and popularity.

"In this portrait, you have received both an invitation to follow God's ways and a warning of the disaster that awaits those who do not. Choose His exceptional way of love."

> 4.3.2. *Jesus teaches about showing love, mercy, and hesitation to judge others (6:27-38).*

²⁷"For those of you who are eager to hear how God would have you live, I share the following truths with you so that you might put them into practice. Here are four concrete actions that you should do:

1. Love your enemies.
2. Do good to those who hate you.
3. ²⁸Speak a blessing on those who speak curses on you (and by "blessing," I do not mean to do it half-heartedly but to actually and genuinely ask God to give His divine favor to them).
4. Pray for the wellbeing of those who are abusing, hurting, or mistreating you.

²⁹"To give you an idea of what these things look like in practice, let Me share four scenarios with you.

1. If someone slaps you on one cheek in rejection, do not be afraid to be vulnerable and offer them the other cheek to hit as well.
2. If someone takes away your coat, do not be afraid to be vulnerable and offer them your shirt as well.
3. ³⁰If someone asks you for something, do not be afraid to be vulnerable and give them what they ask for.
4. If someone is trying to take unfair advantage of you and attempting to take away your belongings, do not be afraid to be vulnerable and let those belongings be taken without trying to get them back.

³¹"You are getting the general idea here, right? Living a life that embodies God's love, humility, and mercy is what matters; it is how to live in the world. But to make this point clear, let Me give you a basic rule of thumb that summarizes this perspective on life. How do you want others to treat you? Figure that out and then take the initiative to be that way for them first. Or to say it in one sentence: Do to others what you would have them do to you.

³²"Now, to make sure you get the point, let Me ask you a series of three questions:

1. If you only love those who love you, how "godly" are you being? Even the ungodly find it easy to love those who love them.
2. ³³If you only do good for those who do good for you, how "godly" are you being? Even the ungodly can do that.
3. ³⁴If you only lend money to those who you know can repay you, how "godly" are you being? Even the ungodly will lend money to people they know will repay them.

³⁵"Do you get it? God calls you to demonstrate an extraordinary kind of love. He calls you to live a life that: 1) loves your enemies, 2) shows everyone kindness and does good things for them, and 3) lends money without expecting anything in return. When you love others in this way, as God would have you do, your reward will be great and you will be living lives that reflect you are children of the Highest Being in Existence. For God is kind, generous, and gracious to those who are ungrateful, selfish, and sinful. ³⁶Just as God is gracious, merciful, and kind, your life should show that you are a child of His by also demonstrating grace, mercy, and kindness to others.

³⁷"When your life imitates God, it benefits you. When your life reflects more grace than judgment toward others, God will not find much to judge in you. When your life embodies more love than condemnation toward others, God will not find much to condemn in you. When your life demonstrates forgiveness toward others, God will forgive much in you. ³⁸When your life acts in generous giving toward others, God will give generously to you. With God, He is like a divine, generous grain merchant in the marketplace. When the divine, generous grain merchant fills your container with grain, He does not leave gaps. Instead, He shakes the container, which levels the grain out so He can put more grain in. This divine, generous grain merchant makes sure you get as much grain as possible and keeps filling your container up until it overflows. Life will be like that for you. When you live with abundant generosity toward others, God will give abundant generosity to you."

### 4.3.3. Jesus teaches about living right with God, bearing the fruit of one's faith, and building one's life on a wise foundation (6:39-49).

³⁹Then Jesus told them a parable—a story illustrating a larger moral point—warning them about following the wrong religious leaders: "Can a blind person lead others who are blind along the right path? If they do, they will most certainly stray from the path and fall into a treacherous pit, right? ⁴⁰A learner—a disciple—does not have more subject knowledge than their teacher. And every student who is fully trained and actively engaged in learning will become like their teacher. So, make sure you are following the right teacher, one who is not spiritually blind."

⁴¹Then He shared another parable with them: "Why do you worry about a speck of dust in your friend's eye when you have an entire tree log in your own eye? ⁴²Why do you have the super-spiritual nerve to say, 'Friend, you are in a dire health situation because you have a speck of sawdust in your eye,' when you are the one who is in a far worse health situation by having a tree log in your own eye? You are a hypocrite that holds a double standard. First, examine yourself and get rid of the tree log in your own eye. Then, you will have the proper perspective that allows you to see clearly how to remove the speck of dust in your friend's eye.

⁴³"So, how do you think we can know the true spiritual character of a person? A good tree does not produce bad fruit; likewise, a bad tree does not produce good fruit. ⁴⁴Every tree is recognized by the fruit it produces. We do not pick apples from thornbushes or grapes from briers. ⁴⁵Similarly, a good person generates good things from the treasury of good that is stored up in their heart. Likewise, an evil person produces evil things from the treasury of evil that is stored up in their heart. And keep in mind that what the mouth speaks merely reveals what is stored up in the treasury of one's heart.

⁴⁶"Now, I must challenge you to follow My teaching and put into practice what I say. Many will call out to Me, 'Lord, Lord,' and claim to believe in Me, but they do not do what I say. ⁴⁷Let Me show you what someone's life looks like when they come to Me, hear My words, and

put them into practice. ⁴⁸That person is like one who built a house on a solid foundation, digging down deep to build on a solid, reliable foundation of rock. And when the rushing water from the floods of life and the storms of living came, they could not shake the house because of it being built on a solid foundation; it had been built to last. ⁴⁹However, let Me share with you what someone's life looks like who does not put my teaching into practice. That person is like a one who built a house on the ground and did not dig any foundation at all. When the rushing water from the floods of life and the storms of living came against that house, it utterly collapsed and was completely destroyed."

> **4.4. Jesus shows that faith in Him is the way to experience salvation (7:1–8:3).**
>
> > *4.4.1. Jesus demonstrates that faith in Him has the authority to heal and that He has power over all things, even death (7:1–17).*

## CHAPTER 7

¹After Jesus had finished teaching all the people on the plain, He entered Capernaum. ²There, a high-ranking Roman military official had a highly valued servant who was very sick and on the verge of death. ³Even though he was not Jewish, the Roman military official had heard of what Jesus had been doing in the area and had respect for Him. Out of concern for his valued servant's life, the Roman military official sent a delegation of Jewish civil leaders to Jesus. He sent them to ask Jesus to come and heal his servant.

⁴When the delegation reached Jesus, they plead with Him to help the servant, saying, "If there is anyone worthy of Your help, this man is. ⁵He has shown great love for the Jewish people and helped build our synagogue."

⁶Jesus responded by going with them. When they were not far from the house, the Roman military official sent a second delegation of his friends to Jesus with a request from the military official. They said, "Lord, I do not want to trouble You or take up any more of Your time. I am just a non-Jewish Roman soldier who is not worthy to be in Your presence nor to have You in my house. ⁷I am not worthy to even meet

You in person, which is why I did not visit You myself. I do not want to be a burden to You, but I believe in Your power, authority, and ability. You can just say the word, and my servant will be healed. [8]As a military leader, I am someone who can appreciate Your power and authority. In my military position, I have certain degree of authority and have over one-thousand soldiers who are under my authority. If I tell one solider to, 'Go,' he goes. If I tell another one, 'Come,' he comes. If I tell my servant, 'Do this,' he does it. So, Lord, You can just speak Your word, and I know my servant will be healed."

[9]When Jesus heard these things, He was surprised and marveled at the Roman military official. Then, Jesus turned to the crowd following Him and said, "You all should pay attention to what just happened here. I have not come across, heard about, or seen a faith as great as this Gentile man's faith in all of Israel."

[10]When the Roman military official's friends returned to his house, they found the servant had been completely healed.

[11]Not long after this happened, Jesus traveled to the town of Nain, which was about twenty miles southwest of Capernaum. Jesus' disciples and a large crowd of followers traveled with Him. [12]As Jesus approached the town's entrance, He came across a funeral procession. The only son of a widow had died, which would leave her all alone and in need of both protection and financial help to get by. A large crowd from the town accompanied her in the funeral procession. [13]When the Lord saw her, He felt deep compassion toward her. Jesus said to her, "Dear woman, let Me put an end to your crying."

[14]Then Jesus walked over to the burial plank on which they were carrying the dead body wrapped in linen. Even though touching the burial plank would make Jesus ceremonially unclean for a period of time according to Jewish traditions, He was more concerned about showing compassion, so He touched the burial plank to stop them. The pallbearers stopped. Then Jesus said, "Young man, I say to you, get up. Arise from death and come back to life again." [15]At that moment, the dead young man sat up and began to talk to Jesus! Jesus then presented him to his mother, and they embraced.

¹⁶A mixture of great fear and profound awe swept the crowd as they realized they were in the presence of profound spiritual power. They responded by praising God, even though they still not understand the truth of Jesus' identity. "We have not seen or heard of such great works of God since the time of Elijah and Elisha. Apparently, a great prophet like them has risen among us! God has come once again to help His people!"

¹⁷The irony was that the Gentile soldier understood Jesus' identity while the Jewish people failed to understand. Even so, the news about what Jesus had done spread throughout Judea and the surrounding countryside.

> 4.4.2. Jesus teaches that faith in Him is the way to God's salvation, not trusting in social, political, or military power (7:18–35).

¹⁸Even though John the Baptist was in prison, John's disciples kept him up-to-date on all the things Jesus had been doing. Everything Jesus was doing fulfilled prophecies from the Old Covenant Scriptures, but John the Baptist had some doubts because what Jesus was doing did not perfectly match John's preconceived expectations of the Messiah—that He should be acting right now as a powerful, sovereign judge who would release God's people from political captivity. So, John summoned two of his disciples. ¹⁹He sent them to inquire of the Lord, "Are you the Anointed One from God—the Messiah who will deliver God's people from their captivity—that we have been waiting for, or should we be waiting for someone else to come?"

²⁰When John's two disciples came to Jesus, they said to Jesus, "John the Baptist sent us to you to ask a question: 'Are you the Anointed One from God—the Messiah who will deliver God's people from their captivity—that we have been waiting for, or should we be waiting for someone else to come?'"

²¹Over the next few hours, Jesus performed many powerful acts of healing. He cured many people of their diseases, their distressing body ailments, and the evil spirits plaguing them. He restored sight to many who were blind. ²²Then, Jesus replied to John the Baptist's messengers:

"Go back and tell John what you have just seen and heard. As the Scriptures of Isaiah foretold: The blind can see, the lame can walk, the lepers are cleansed, the deaf can hear, the dead are raised to life, and God's good news message of salvation is preached to the poor. ²³And tell him that the truly fortunate ones before God are those who are not offended, who do not turn away, and who do not stumble in their faith because My humble, servant-oriented way of doing things are different than what they may have expected."

²⁴After John the Baptist's messengers left, Jesus took the opportunity to highlight the two different eras of God's work that were happening among God's people. Jesus said, "When you went out into the wilderness to hear John the Baptist, what did you see? Did you go out to the Jordan River Valley just to see reeds swaying in the wind, just to enjoy the scenery? ²⁵No? Then maybe you went out there to see his fabulous fashion? That is extremely unlikely because those wearing the most expensive, most fashionable clothes do not wear them in the wilderness. Those types usually hang out in places of luxury and live in palaces. ²⁶So, with John the Baptist, what did you go out there to see? Were you looking for a prophet delivering a message from God? Yes, of course you were. And you did not see any ordinary prophet; you saw a particularly special prophet.

²⁷"John is the one the Scriptures spoke of in Malachi 3:1, where it is written,

> Pay special attention to the messenger I am sending ahead of God's Anointed Deliverer.
> He will prepare a smooth, straight, and clear path for God's people to receive Him.

²⁸"And I am telling you this truth: among all of the people born before this new era of God's work that is now working among you, no one has been more important or greater than John the Baptist. However, do you realize that in this new era of God's work among you, even the person of lowest status in God's kingdom is greater than the most significant person of the old era? The greatest person in the old era does not even compare to the lowest person in the new era of God's kingdom!"

²⁹When everyone there heard Jesus say these things, it produced the typical reaction. The ordinary, everyday people—including those considered normal, everyday sinners, such as tax collectors—acknowledged that God's way was right and turned their hearts and mind toward following Him. They had been baptized by John the Baptist as an outward, symbolic act to demonstrate their inward faith in God's coming kingdom. ³⁰But the religious leaders—the Pharisees and the recognized experts in the religious law—rejected God's plan of salvation and His purpose for them. They did not recognize their need to repent of their sin and turn back to God. As a result, they saw no need to be baptized by John and refused it.

³¹Jesus continued to teach them, "To what can I compare an entire generation of these so-called 'recognized religious leaders and experts?' ³²They are like spoiled, bratty children playing a game in the public market. They bicker, gripe, and whine to each other:

> We played happy music for you,
> > but you did not dance for us the way that we wanted you to;
> We played sappy songs for you,
> > but you did not get sad or weep for us the way we wanted you to.

³³ "When John the Baptist arrived and fasted from bread and wine, you said, 'He is demon-possessed.' ³⁴When the Son of Man arrived and feasted on bread and wine, you said, 'He is a drunkard out of control, and He has so many questionable friendships with despised tax collectors and other notorious sinners.' ³⁵This generation of so-called 'recognized religious leaders and experts' can whine like spoiled, bratty children all they want. But in the end, genuine godly wisdom will prove itself; it will be shown to be true in the lives of those who follow it."

> 4.4.3. *Jesus identifies that a humble, trusting faith in Him is the way to experience God's forgiveness, not following the legalistic letter of religious teachings (7:36–8:3).*

³⁶Later on, one of the Pharisees asked Jesus to have dinner with him.

Jesus went to the Pharisee's home and sat down at the dinner table in the typical reclining position. ³⁷When a woman known socially as living a sinful life learned that Jesus was eating at the Pharisee's house, she came to the house, motivated by faith. As was the custom, when someone had dinner with a well-known public figure like Jesus, the host often left the doors open so that others could also enter, sit along the edge of the room, and hear what was said. Intending to honor Jesus, this woman known for sinful living came to the dinner; she brought with her a very expensive jar of perfume, which was likely worth more than half a year's wages or more. ³⁸As she stood behind Jesus near His feet, she wept. Her tears began to fall on His feet and wet them. She wiped her tears from His feet with her hair. She then honored who Jesus was by humbly greeting Him with a kiss on His feet and pouring the expensive perfume on them.

³⁹When the Pharisee who had invited Jesus to the dinner saw this, he was disturbed. He thought to himself, "If this guy was really a prophet from God, He would have known what kind of woman is touching Him and not allowed it, for she is widely known all over town for her sinful behavior."

⁴⁰Jesus replied, "Simon, I have a story to share with you, if you would like to hear it."

He replied, "Sure, tell me."

⁴¹"Two people owed money to a moneylender. One person owed twenty-four months of full-time wages; the other person owed two months of full-time wages. ⁴²Unfortunately, neither of these people could repay their loans. But the moneylender canceled out and forgave the debts of both. Now, which of these two debtors do you think will be more grateful for their debt being forgiven?"

⁴³Simon answered, "I suppose the one who had the bigger debt canceled and forgiven."

Jesus responded, "You are absolutely right!"

⁴⁴Then Jesus turned toward the woman while He was speaking to

Simon and said, "Simon, do you see this woman? When I entered your house, you gave Me no water to cleanse My feet because you were not required to by custom. But this woman, motivated by grateful love, washed My feet with her own hair and with her tears that wet My feet. [45]You did not greet Me socially with a kiss of greeting because you were not required to by custom. But this woman, motivated by grateful love, did not hesitate to greet Me with a humble kiss of greeting on My feet. [46]You did not give Me any oil to freshen up with because you were not required to by custom. But this woman, motivated by grateful love, honored Me and soothed My feet by pouring an expense perfume on them.

[47]"Therefore, let Me tell you a deeper truth about this situation: this woman realized her need for forgiveness from her many sins. Her grateful, loving actions reflect that she knows what it is like to be forgiven from them. But the opposite is also true: whoever does not realize their need for forgiveness from their sin has been forgiven little. And by virtue of knowing little about receiving forgiveness, they show little grateful love in return."

[48]Then Jesus said to the woman, "You have already demonstrated that you know the forgiveness that comes through faith in Me, but just to make sure you know, let Me tell you clearly: your sins are forgiven."

[49]The Pharisee's guests at the dinner table murmured among themselves, "Who does this guy think He is? He associates with a sinner, and now He thinks He can forgive sins? God alone can forgive sins! How arrogant and blasphemous He is to make a statement like that."

[50]Then Jesus said to the woman, "Your faith has saved you; you can go forward through life in peace."

## CHAPTER 8

[1]After this event, Jesus traveled through various towns and villages, proclaiming the good news of God's kingdom. The twelve apostles traveled with Him, but the good news of God's kingdom is not bound by any racial, political, and social class, nor is it only experienced by males. [2]Many women traveled with Jesus who had been

healed of various evil afflictions and diseases. Among them were Mary Magdalene, who had seven demons cast out; ³Joanna, who was of higher social and financial status than most because she was the wife of Chuza, Herod's business manager; Susanna; and many others. They all were helping support Jesus' ministry by giving of their own personal means.

### 4.5. Jesus shows what faith in Him looks like by calling on His disciples to trust in Him and His Word (8:4–9:17).

*4.5.1 Jesus teaches that people must respond to His Word with faith (8:4–21).*

4.5.1a. Jesus teaches that faith should be an ongoing, continuous, nurturing reality in one's life (8:4-15).

⁴One day, people from various towns had gathered around Jesus and formed a great crowd. Jesus taught them through a parable: ⁵"A farmer went out to sow some seed. As he was scattering seed, some feel on the road. It was trampled on, and the birds came and devoured it. ⁶Other seed fell on rocky ground, where rocks lie underneath a thin layer of topsoil. The seed sprouted initially but soon withered away because it did not have good roots. ⁷Other seed fell among thorns. As it sprouted and grew, it was strangled from life by the other plants. ⁸Yet other seed fell on fertile soil. This seed kept on sprouting, growing, and increasing the harvest. It produced a yield that was a hundred times what was sown, vastly surpassing the seven to tenfold yield that would typically be expected." After Jesus told them the parable, He challenged them, "Whoever has ears to hear, they should use them to listen and understand."

⁹Later, Jesus' disciples asked Him what the parable meant. ¹⁰Jesus said, "God has given to you an understanding of His revealed truth about the kingdom of God. But to others—those who are not seeking an understanding—religious truth becomes a mysterious riddle that they give up on. These others who are not seeking or who give up on seeking God's truth are described in Isaiah 6:9:

> Though they see, they never comprehend;
> Though they hear, they never learn.

¹¹"Now, let Me share with you the meaning of this parable. The seed is the Word of God, His revealed truth. ¹²The seed on the road represents those who hear God's Word but allow the devil to come and carry the message away from their hearts so that they may not believe in Me and be saved. ¹³The seed on the rocky ground signifies those who immediately receive God's Word with joy when they hear it. However, they never allow the Word to establish deep roots within them or change their lives. As a result, they believe for a little while, but when their belief is tested or tempted, they fall away. ¹⁴The seed that fell among the thorns represents those who hear God's Word very receptively. But as they go through life, the desires for the riches and pleasures of this life dominate their minds; they do not mature in the faith to produce fruit. ¹⁵Yet the seeds that fell on the fertile soil characterize those who hear God's Word receptively, allow it take root inside them, hold on to it with an honest and good heart, preserve through whatever seasons may come, and see it mature by faith and produce fruit over time.

> 4.5.1.a. Jesus teaches that people must respond to the light of His Word with faith (8:16-21).

¹⁶"While one should respond to God's Word not just for a few moments but instead continually cultivate and nurture His Word, one should also recognize that God's Word is a constant light that shines into our lives. Think about it. No one would light a lamp just to cover it up with a dark jar or hide it under the bed where it cannot be seen. Instead, a lamp is put on a stand so that anyone who comes into the room may see its light. ¹⁷Things are only temporarily concealed. God is hiding nothing except only what He intends to reveal later. God is not hiding any secret that He will not bring out into the full, open, and clear light. ¹⁸So pay attention and use your ears to hear and understand. To those who are listening and learning, they will be given more knowledge and understanding. However, for those who are not listening and learning, even what little understanding they have will be taken away."

¹⁹Then, Jesus' mother and brothers came to see Him. However, they could not get close to Jesus because of the size of the crowd around Him. ²⁰His family sent a message to Him, "Your mother and brothers are standing outside; they want to see You and desire You to go home with them, stopping Your ministry before it disturbs the world."

²¹But Jesus replied, "My true mother and brothers—My real and lasting family—are those who learn God's Word and put it into practice."

> 4.5.2. *Jesus teaches that His followers can trust Him to care for their best interests, no matter what storms may come in their lives, and that He has power and authority over nature [Miracle 1: The Stilling of the Storm] (8:22-25).*

²²One day, Jesus said to His disciples, "Let us go over to the other side of the lake." So, they all got into a boat and set out. ²³As they sailed, Jesus fell asleep. While He was sleeping, a furious storm of hurricane proportions came down the hills and upon the lake. High, strong waves began to fill the boat with water. Even the experienced fishermen felt they were in grave danger.

²⁴The disciples went to Jesus and woke Him up, saying, "Master, Master, we are going to die out here!"

Jesus awoke and rebuked the wind and the raging waters. At His word, the storm completely stopped, and everything was calm. ²⁵Jesus asked them, "Where is your faith? Do you not trust that God will take care of you?"

With a mixture of fear and awe-filled amazement, they asked one another, "Who is this man? Even the wind and the waves obey Him."

> 4.5.3. *Jesus teaches how people can have a variety of responses to Him, and that He has power and authority over demonic power [Miracle 2: Jesus exorcises demons] (8:26-39).*

²⁶Then they sailed on to the region of the Gerasenes, a non-Jewish area across the lake from Galilee. ²⁷When Jesus stepped out onto land, a demon-possessed man from the city met Him. For a long time, this man had not worn clothes nor lived in a house. He was known for living among the tombs. ²⁸When the demon-possessed man saw Jesus, he cried out in a loud voice, fell before Jesus, and said loudly, "Why are you interfering with me by your presence here, Jesus, Son of the Most

High God?" But when calling Jesus' name out and recognizing His identity did not give him the upper hand in the spiritual confrontation, the demon turned to begging, "I beg you, please do not torture me!" ²⁹The demon begged because Jesus had just commanded the unclean, evil spirits to come out of the man. These unclean, evil spirits had made this man uncontrollable. Many times, various people tried to confine the demon-possessed man with chains binding his hands and locking the shackles around his feet. But the demon-possessed man would tear and break them apart. These demons also drove this man into the isolated wilderness and to the outskirts of society.

³⁰Then Jesus asked the demon-possessed man, "Demon, what is your name?"

He replied, "Legion," because about as many demons as a legion of 6,000 soldiers and 120 horsemen had gone into this man. ³¹The demons knew Jesus overpowered them. They begged Him to not cast them out into the isolated sea or some deep, desolate pit.

³²There happened to be a large heard of pigs feeding on the hillside. The demons begged Jesus to let them go into the pigs. Jesus gave them permission. ³³Then the demons came out of the man and entered the pigs. When they did, the entire herd of pigs went crazy. In a mania, they rushed down the steep bank and plunged themselves into the lake to drown. ³⁴When those who had been feeding the pigs saw the event, they ran away and told everyone in the town and on every farm along the countryside what had happened.

³⁵Then people rushed out to see what had happened for themselves. As they approached Jesus, they saw the man who had been possessed by a legion of demons sitting at Jesus' feet. The formerly demon-possessed man was dressed and in his right mind. Knowing that a mighty spiritual power of some sort was in their presence, they were terrified. ³⁶Those who had been eyewitnesses to the entire event with the demon-possessed man told how he had been healed. ³⁷Yet the people were overcome with fear of Jesus' spiritual power and responded negatively. All the people of the region begged Jesus to leave them alone. So, Jesus got back in the boat, left them, and returned to the other side of the lake.

³⁸The man who had been delivered from the demons pleaded with Jesus, asking to go with Him. But Jesus redirected the man and said, ³⁹"I appreciate your desire to go with us. But now you are free from the demons and no longer a lonely outcast from society. Instead of coming with us, go home to your family. Be with them and tell them everything God has done for you." The man did as he was told. He left there and began telling everyone he came across how much Jesus had done for him.

> 4.5.4. *Jesus teaches that sometimes faith needs bolstering and encouragement, while other times it needs calm, persistent trusting, and that He has power and authority over disease and death [Miracles 3 and 4: A healing and a resuscitation from the dead] (8:40–56).*

⁴⁰When Jesus had crossed back across the lake to Galilee, a large crowd was waiting there to welcome Him. ⁴¹Then a man named Jairus, who was one of the leaders in the Jewish synagogue, approached Jesus. He fell at Jesus' feet and begged Him to come to his house. ⁴²Jairus was desperate for Jesus' help because his twelve-year-old daughter was dying.

As Jesus walked with Jairus, the large crowd around them was packed so tightly that it was almost suffocating. ⁴³In the crowd, there was a woman who had been suffering from an abnormal uterine and vaginal bleeding for twelve years. Because of this condition, she had suffered socially (being labeled unclean from the bleeding), physically, and financially. She had sought help all over, yet no one could heal her. ⁴⁴She believed Jesus was so powerful that she could be healed just by touching His clothes. As they walked, she slipped up behind Jesus and touched the outer edge of His coat. Immediately, her bleeding stopped.

⁴⁵Jesus realized what had happened, and He turned to the crowd, asking, "Who was it? Who touched Me?"

When everyone denied having touched Him intentionally, Peter said to Him, "Master, why are You worried about one person touching You? The crowd is packed so tightly that they are almost crushing us.

Hundreds of people are touching You as You pass by. Why are You concerned about one person touching You?"

⁴⁶But Jesus did not relent and said, "Someone here touched Me and was healed, for I felt My healing power work on them."

⁴⁷The woman knew she could no longer go unnoticed. Fearful of what Jesus might say or what the people might think, she came forward, trembling, and fell at Jesus' feet. In front of the entire crowd, she explained her motive, why she had touched Jesus, and how she was healed instantly. ⁴⁸Then Jesus said to her, "Daughter, let Me reassure you, your faith in Me has healed you. You do not need to hide your actions prompted by faith; you can be confident in them. And may the full and complete peace of God, which infiltrates every aspect of your life, be with you as you go."

⁴⁹While Jesus was still talking, a person arrived from the house of Jairus, the synagogue leader. He said, "Unfortunately, your daughter is dead, and there is no use in troubling the Teacher anymore."

⁵⁰Overhearing the conversation, Jesus said to Jairus, "Do not be alarmed by what they are telling you. Just keep on trusting in Me, and she will be healed."

⁵¹When they arrived at Jairus' house, Jesus went inside. He would not let anyone from the crowd go in with Him except Peter, John, James, and the child's father and mother. ⁵²As they entered, everyone inside the house was weeping and morning the girl's death. Jesus said to them, "There is no need for all your weeping. This girl is not dead, just asleep."

⁵³All the people inside the house laughed at Jesus' comment because they knew first-hand that the girl was dead. ⁵⁴Then Jesus reached out, taking the dead girl's limp hand, and said to her, "Little girl, arise from your death." ⁵⁵At that moment, life came back into the girl's dead body. She immediately rose up. Then Jesus instructed them to give her something to eat so that people would know she was physically alive and well. ⁵⁶Her parents were overwhelmed with amazement. Yet Jesus did not want this girl's resuscitation to feed the growing frenzy of His

reputation as a miracle worker. So, He gave the parents clear directions not to tell anyone what had happened in the child's room and how she had been brought back to life.

> 4.5.5. *Jesus teaches that the message of the arrival of His kingdom is a message of hope that should be spread and shared with everyone (9:1-9).*

## CHAPTER 9

¹One day, as the opposition to Jesus grew, and because He desired to expand the radius of His message and ministry to reach more people, He called His twelve appointed apostles together. He wanted to prepare them to go out an act as His officially commissioned ambassadors. To do so, Jesus gave them some of the same power He had—the power and authority to drive out any demon and heal any disease. ²He sent them to proclaim the arrival of God's kingdom publicly and to heal the sick. ³ Jesus instructed them: "As you go, rely and depend on the generosity of others. Take nothing with you for your journey—no walking stick, no packed bags, no food, no money, and no extra clothing. ⁴Whenever you find someone willing to let you stay at their house, stay in that location the whole time until you are ready to leave that town. Do not try to upgrade to someone else's nicer home, as it communicates the wrong thing to the people whom you are there to serve. ⁵You will be presenting a message that calls people to make a clear choice about their lives. Anticipate both positive and negative responses. If any place does not welcome you or listen to you, it is okay to leave that town. Simply shake the dust off your sandaled feet, which symbolically communicates that you are no longer associated with that town and that those people have been abandoned to their fate before God." ⁶After being commissioned, the twelve disciples who were appointed apostles went outward—traveling from town to town, publicly proclaiming the good news that God's kingdom had arrived in Jesus and healing people everywhere they went.

⁷As the news about Jesus spread, everyone heard about it, including the highest social circle in the region—the court of Herod Antipas, the Roman governor of Judea. When Herod Antipas heard about what Jesus was doing, he was perplexed and troubled by the news. Herod heard that some people believed Jesus was John the Baptist raised from

the dead. ⁸He heard that others believed Jesus was the major, powerful prophet Elijah from the Old Covenant Scriptures who had reappeared from heaven. And he heard that others believed Jesus was one of the other prophets of the Old Covenant Scriptures who had come back to life. ⁹Herod, not knowing what to make of the situation, said, "I beheaded John the Baptist, so I do not know who this man could be that I have been hearing so much about? I wonder who He is?" And Herod kept looking for a chance to see Him.

> 4.5.6. *Jesus teaches that He will provide for the needs of His followers (9:10–17).*

¹⁰When the apostles returned from their journey, they reported to Jesus what they had done. Then, He slipped away with them to take a retreat in a town called Bethsaida. ¹¹However, the crowds found out where Jesus was going, and they followed Him there. As they approached Him, Jesus welcomed them graciously, taught them about the kingdom of God, and healed the sick who needed it.

¹²As it got later in the day, the twelve apostles came to Jesus and said, "It is getting late. You may want to send these people away now so that they still have a chance to making it to the surrounding villages and countryside to find food and lodging for the night. After all, we are in a remote, isolated place."

¹³But Jesus replied to them, "Why should we send them away at all? How about you twelve apostles give them something to eat?"

They responded, "We do not have the supplies to feed that many people. We only have five loaves of bread and two fish. We would have to go buy a huge amount of food to feed this crowd." ¹⁴About 5,000 men were there (and that count did not include their families).

Jesus told His disciples, "It is not necessary to buy more food. Just split this crowd into groups of around fifty people each, and let us see what I can do for them."

¹⁵The disciples split the crowd up as instructed and had them sit down. ¹⁶Then Jesus took the five loaves of bread and two fish in His hands.

He looked up to heaven, gave thanks to God for His provision, and began breaking the food into portions. As He prepared the meal, Jesus kept on providing food to the disciples to distribute to the people and never ran out. [17]Everyone in the vast crowd of people ate as much as they wanted, eating until they were satisfied. As the disciples were cleaning up after the meal, they picked up twelve large basketfuls of leftovers. Jesus had just evoked images of the great Messianic banquet where all of God's people will enjoy the perfect community and gracious provision of the Messiah's salvation. But not only had Jesus demonstrated that His provision meets everyone's needs, He had also shown His disciples that God's provision could come through them—that God can accomplish His work in the world through the work He gives His people to do.

### 4.6. Responding to Jesus through faith: One must confess trust in Christ and continue to live by faith in Him daily (9:18–50).

*4.6.1. Faith in Jesus requires confessing complete trust in Christ, who He is, and the salvation He brings to His people (9:18–22).*

[18]One day, Jesus was praying alone with His disciples nearby. He approached them and asked, "Who do the crowds say I am?"

[19]They answered, "Some say John the Baptist returned to life. Some say Elijah returned from heaven. Others say one of the prophets of old that has been raised back to life."

[20]"But what about you?" Jesus asked them. "Who do you say I am?"

Peter answered, "The Christ from God, the Anointed One who will decisively deliver His people."

[21]Knowing the inherent danger in the public's misunderstanding of His identity, Jesus strictly warned His disciples not to tell anyone about Him being the Messiah. [22]Then, building on their fundamental and foundational understanding of God's plan, Jesus taught them more about His identity and mission, saying, "The Son of Man must

suffer many terrible things and be completely rejected by the so-called wise leaders, chief priests, and teachers of the Jewish law. He will be killed, but on the third day, He will be raised up from the dead."

> 4.6.2. *Faith in Jesus requires a continual and daily commitment to following Him (9:23-27).*

²³Then Jesus said to them, "If anyone wants to be My follower, they must lose sight of themselves and say no to their own interests, they must take up their cross on a daily basis as one prepared to face rejection from the world and live as one dead to the world's values and lifestyles, and they must follow Me every day and from now on in the way of life. ²⁴Following My teaching and My way of life to attain security and a holistic, fulfilling, and God-honoring life presents one with a great paradox. For whoever tries to save their life by following their own way will lose their life, but whoever loses their life to follow My teaching and My way of life will actually save it. ²⁵No matter who a person is, what good is it to gain all the esteem, power, and wealth of the world in an attempt to secure life now—if by doing so you stray from following God's way and forfeit your very soul and life in God's kingdom? ²⁶There is an eternal judgment that is coming. If anyone is ashamed to follow Me and My teaching, then the Son of Man will be ashamed of that person when He comes, with the holy angels, in His Father's full glory.

²⁷Even though this road of discipleship—following Me and learning My teaching and ways—is hard, it has divine benefits and rewards. I tell you this truth: some are standing here right now who will not experience death before they get a first-hand, up-close glimpse into the fullness of the kingdom of God."

> 4.6.3. *Faith in Jesus requires listening to Him and recognizing the ongoing need to listen to Him (9:28-36).*

²⁸About eight days later, Jesus took Peter, John, and James with Him on a prayer retreat up on a mountain. ²⁹While Jesus was praying, the appearance of His face transformed. His clothes changed into a dazzling white that looked as bright as a flash of lightning. ³⁰All of a sudden, two men appeared with Him in the same transformed appearance

that Jesus had. These two men were Moses and Elijah, and they represented the hope of God's fulfilled promises that span the early and late periods of the Old Covenant's history. ³¹They were discussing Jesus' exodus, His departure from this world, which was about to be accomplished in Jerusalem.

³²As this conversation was taking place, Peter and those around him were asleep. But when they woke up, they saw Jesus in His glory and the two men standing there with Him. ³³As Moses and Elijah were about to leave, Peter did not know what to say. He understood that Moses' and Elijah's presence there signified the hope and fulfillment of God's promises and highlighted how Jesus would be the fulfillment of that hope. Not knowing what else to do, Peter asked if he could honor them and the significance of their gathering: "Master, it is so amazing and beautiful for us to be here! In honor of this special occasion and the hope that it represents, let us build three tents—one for You, one for Moses, and one for Elijah."

³⁴But even as Peter was speaking, a cloud radiating a brilliant light appeared that surrounded and overshadowed them. As the cloud of light covered them, the disciples recalled how God spoke through clouds in the Old Covenant Scriptures, and they became terribly afraid. ³⁵Then a voice came out of the cloud, saying, "This is My Son, the One whom I have chosen to work through. Listen to Him." ³⁶When the voice had finished speaking, the transcendent summit was over, and everything disappeared. Jesus, no longer in a transformed appearance, was left standing there alone. But the point was clear: even though they had a foundational understanding of who Jesus was, the disciples needed—and we must continually—to listen to Jesus. And after this event concluded, these three disciples kept what had happened to themselves; they did not tell anyone what they had seen until God's full plan had unfolded.

> 4.6.4. *Faith in Jesus requires trusting in His power at work in our lives, not relying on our means and power, and recognizing that He is calling people from all walks of life to follow and serve Him (9:37–50).*

³⁷The next day, as they were coming down from the mountain, a large

crowd was there to meet them. ³⁸A man from the crowd called out to Jesus, "Teacher, I beg you to take a look at my son, for he is my only child. ³⁹An evil spirit keeps seizing him, causing him to scream, go into violent convulsions, and to foam at the mouth. This evil spirit beats him up and hardly ever leaves him alone. ⁴⁰I pleaded with Your disciples to drive it out, but, by their own power, they could not do it."

⁴¹Jesus replied, "What a faithless and unbelieving generation! Time is running short, and how long do I need to stay with you in this world for you to see God's bigger purpose? How long shall I put up with you not understanding God's purpose for life and His ways? Bring your boy here to Me."

⁴²While the boy was coming, the demon threw him to the ground in a violent convulsion. But Jesus rebuked the unclean, evil spirit, healed the boy, and handed him back to his father.

⁴³Everyone there was astonished at the majestic display of God's mighty power they had just witnessed.

While everyone was still marveling at what He was doing, Jesus said to His disciples, ⁴⁴"Listen carefully to what I am about to tell you and let these words really sink in: the Son of Man is going to be betrayed and delivered into the hands of His enemies."

⁴⁵But the disciples did not understand what He meant. What Jesus said about the Son of Man's betrayal was not in the realm of what they thought possible for the Messiah. They thought the Messiah would be a present, political, religious, and military leader who would win a decisive victory over the world. What Jesus told them did not make any sense to them. But they were afraid to look incompetent, so they did not ask Him about it.

⁴⁶As they were traveling, an argument broke out among the disciples about who would be the greatest in God's kingdom, who would have the highest status. ⁴⁷Jesus, perceiving their thoughts and ambitions, took a little child and had him stand by His side.

⁴⁸Then He said to His disciples, "Whoever receives a seemingly

powerless, irrelevant, and socially unimportant child into their home, actually welcomes Me. And whoever receives Me into their home actually welcomes the Father who sent Me. Among My followers, those with the least social standing among you who believes in Me shares the same spiritual status as the ones among you perceive as those holding the greatest social standing. Among My followers, these types of differences are obliterated: all who receive Me are made great!"

[49]On a different topic, John raised a concern to Jesus: "Master, we saw someone casting out demons in Your name. We tried to stop him because he was not one of your authorized representatives actively following You."

[50]But Jesus instructed him, "There is no need to stop him, for we are not trying to keep this work limited to only a select few; we want many others to join us in it. And anyone who is not against you is for you."

## 5. Following the Savior: The life of following Christ is a journey of faith. [The Journey to Jerusalem] (9:51–19:44).

### 5.1. The life of following Christ requires commitment and will include both moments of failure and success (9:51–10:24).

#### 5.1.1. *Following Christ is not a casual affair but requires commitment (9:51–62).*

##### 5.1.1.a. Understand the focus in serving Christ is not on judgment but on grace and sharing His grace with others (9:51-56).

[51]As the days drew near for Jesus' ascension back to heaven, Jesus resolutely focused His travel itinerary and set out on a journey toward one single destination—Jerusalem. [52]As they traveled, Jesus would send His messengers ahead of Him to the next town He was about to visit. They came into a Samaritan village to make arrangements for Jesus' visit. [53]However, the people in the Samaritan village did not offer any hospitality or welcome Jesus because they learned He was just passing through on His way to Jerusalem. [54]When James and John saw what

had happened, they were not pleased. Like the Old Covenant prophet Elijah, they were ready to ask God for the village's instant destruction because of their rejection. They asked, "Lord, shall we call down God's fiery judgment from heaven to destroy these people, just as Elijah did?"

⁵⁵However, Jesus turned to His disciples and severely rebuked them for focusing their ministry on being accepted by others. He reminded them that following Him is not an easy path and will include rejection. He reminded them that they should focus their ministry not on judging those who do not accept Him but instead on sharing His grace with others and solemnly warning those who do not receive Him about their ultimate accountability to God. ⁵⁶After giving His rebuke, Jesus and His disciples continued their one-way journey to Jerusalem by moving on to the next village.

  5.1.1.b. Understand the cost of following Christ (9:57-62).

⁵⁷As they were walking along the road, a person said to Jesus, "I am eager to follow You; I will follow You wherever You go."

⁵⁸But Jesus wanted him to understand what that meant. Jesus said, "Do you understand the commitment that requires? Following Me is not like following an established, institutional religious leader. While foxes have dens and birds have nests, the Son of Man does not have an established, certain place to sleep at night."

⁵⁹To another person on the road, Jesus invited them, saying, "Come, follow Me."

But the person replied, "I would like to, but my father just died. According to Jewish customs, burying a family member is a high-priority. So, let me first go bury my father, then I will come back and follow You."

⁶⁰But Jesus told him, "You should focus on life instead of death. Let the spiritually dead bury their own dead. Proclaiming the kingdom of God, which focuses on life, is to be your highest priority."

⁶¹Another person approached Jesus and said, "I am eager to follow You, Lord, but first, let me turn around and go back to say goodbye to my

family."

⁶²But Jesus told him, "In this rugged terrain, anyone who puts their hand to the plow and turns around to look back risks making mistakes and being dangerously knocked off course. Similarly, anyone who is not forwardly and persistently focused on God's work is not fit for service in His kingdom."

> 5.1.2. Following Christ calls one into God's service, and serving Him will include both moments of failure and success (10:1–24).

## CHAPTER 10

¹Later on, after sharing this teaching, the Lord decided to send out another, larger group of His disciples on a mission. He appointed seventy-two disciples to go out in pairs as an advance team that would go into every town and place that He would pass through on His way to Jerusalem. ²Jesus gave them the following instructions: "As you begin, realize that the harvest is huge; the work to be done is bigger than what the current laborers can possibly accomplish. Therefore, start by asking the Lord—the One who is in charge of the harvest—to send more workers out into the harvest fields. ³Then, go out and serve. But as you labor, remember that the work is not easy; it is dangerous, and you will experience rejection. Remember that I am sending you out to labor like lambs who live among wolves. ⁴To help you be flexible, agile, and focused on God as you journey, travel light. Do not take your moneybag, a backpack, or an extra pair of sandals—be prepared to depend on God and the hospitality of others. Do not spend time making too much small talk with people you meet along the way.

⁵"Whenever you enter someone's house who might be a willing host for you, say, 'May the peace of God fill this place.' ⁶If they respond positively to your blessing on the house, then you know it is an excellent place to stay. However, if they react negatively, then you know it is not a good place to stay. Find a home that will welcome you and God's message. ⁷When you have found a house that welcomes you, stay there. Drink and eat what they give you, for they desire to provide for your labor. Do not move from house to house, trying to find a better home or better provisions.

⁸"Whenever you enter a town and are welcomed there, honor their hospitality by eating what they offer. ⁹But do not lose sight of your main responsibility in that town: to heal the sick and to tell them, 'The kingdom of God is at hand and is now upon you.' ¹⁰However, if you enter a town and you and your message are not welcomed there, then go out into the city center and say, ¹¹'We now wipe the dust of your town from our feet as a symbol that we and God's message are no longer associated with you. It is also a warning that you are accountable to God for rejecting His message. But your rejection does not change the reality of God's kingdom being at hand and now among us. Your rejection just means you are missing out on God's salvation.' ¹²And let Me tell you this sad reality: for those who miss God's kingdom and His salvation, it will be better on God's Judgment Day for the wicked city of Sodom in the Old Covenant Scriptures—which was utterly destroyed—than for a town who rejects the kingdom of God.

¹³"What tragic sorrow awaits the Jewish cities of Chorazin and Bethsaida, cities at the north end of the Sea of Galilee where I spent much time! God's kingdom was powerfully at work among them, yet in their proud opposition to God, they missed it. If the mighty works of God's kingdom that I did there had been done in the evilest of Gentile towns such as Tyre and Sidon—places that Jewish people associate with utter rebellion against God—even those pagan places would have turned to God long ago. They would have felt so much sorrow for their sin that they would have sat in sackcloth and ashes to show their deep remorse and mourning before God. ¹⁴Do you Jewish cities realize that it will be worse for you on God's Judgment Day than it will be for those wicked, evil Gentile towns of Tyre and Sidon? ¹⁵And what about you, the Jewish city of Capernaum? Do you think you will be lifted up to the heavens by default of who you are? Hardly. Instead, you will be brought down into the deepest depths of hell.

¹⁶"You see, there is an unbreakable link that exists here between Me, you, and those people who either listen to or reject your message about God's kingdom. Whoever listens to you and the message you bring is actually listening to Me. Whoever rejects you and the message you bring is actually rejecting Me and rejecting God the Father who sent Me."

[17]When the seventy-two returned, they were joyful and excited. They said, "Lord, even the demons obey us when we live and serve as You would have us to."

[18]Jesus replied, "Indeed, and they will. The power that operates in you is more powerful than the power operating in those demons, for I saw Satan's fall from heaven. The power that banished him caused him to fall so fast it was like lightning flashing across the sky. [19]Now pay particular attention to this: I have given you enough power and authority that no power of the enemy can harm you. With the power and authority I have given you, you can trample on evil as though it were spiritual snakes and scorpions and crush them without any fear of spiritual harm. [20]But do not rejoice and get excited because evil powers submit to you. Instead, you should rejoice and be excited that your names are registered in heaven's census, written on heaven's membership list, indicating that you belong there."

[21]Right after Jesus told them these things, He was filled with the joy of the Holy Spirit and praised God for the successful mission of His followers. He said, "I thank You, Father, the Lord who rules over all of heaven and earth, because You have hidden Your ways from the religious experts and know-it-alls. Instead, You have revealed Your teaching and ways to the simple newcomers who approach You like a little child, to those who trust You with a simple faith. Yes, Father, it pleased You to do everything this way, and I am thankful for it.

[22]"Father, You have entrusted all things to Me. No one can know the fullness of who the Son is except the Father, and no one knows the fullness of who the Father is except the Son. Thankfully, the Son can reveal the Father to anyone the Son chooses."

[23]Then Jesus turned again to the disciples who had just returned. He said to them privately, "Your eyes are extremely fortunate and favored by God because of what they have seen. [24]For I tell you this truth: throughout history, there have been many godly prophets and kings who wanted to see the new era of God's kingdom at work that you have seen, but they did not get to see it. They longed to hear the sound of the new era of God's kingdom at work that you have heard, but they

did not get to hear it."

### 5.2. The life of following Christ influences one's relationships with others (10:25–11:13).

#### 5.2.1. Following Christ requires seeing everyone as a neighbor who should be loved (10:25–37).

$^{25}$One day, an expert in the Jewish religious law stood up and asked Jesus a question in order to test Him and confirm what God's expectations are. He asked, "Teacher, what must I do to ensure I meet God's requirements, experience His salvation, and have eternal life with Him?"

$^{26}$Jesus replied, "When you read the Torah—the first five books of the Old Covenant Scriptures that you are well-versed in—how would you summarize its teaching to answer your own question?"

$^{27}$The man answered, "Two teachings could summarize God's expectations. The first teaching comes from Deuteronomy 6:5, which says, 'Love the love the Lord your God with all your heart, with all your soul, with all your strength, and with all your mind.' The second teaching comes from Leviticus 19:18, which says, 'Love your neighbor as yourself.'"

$^{28}$Then Jesus replied, "That is a very insightful answer; it shows you understand God's fundamental expectations. Do those things, and you will enjoy an everlasting life with God."

$^{29}$But the man wanted more. He wanted to know the scope of the call to love one's neighbor. The man was familiar with the old Jewish practice that identified some people as neighbors (mainly the Jewish people who loved God) and others as non-neighbors (including Gentiles, Samaritans, or other "sinners"). He was hoping to hear Jesus affirm that practice. So, he asked Jesus, "Can you further define who the 'your neighbor' teaching applies to? Does that mean to love everyone, or, as we commonly accept, does that just refer to loving God's people as we love ourselves?"

³⁰Jesus replied to his question with a story: "There once was a man traveling on that dangerous, seventeen-mile stretch of road between Jerusalem and Jericho. During his journey, the man was brutally attacked by ruthless bandits. They stripped him of his clothes, beat him severely, and left him half-dead beside the road. ³¹By coincidence, a Jewish priest happened to be traveling this same road. However, when he saw the beaten, half-dead man, the Jewish priest just crossed over to the other side of the road and passed by him. ³²Likewise, a Levite who assisted in the worship of the Jewish Temple was traveling this road as well. When he came to the place where the beaten, half-dead man lay, the Levite man also crossed over to the other side of the road and passed by him. ³³But then one of those despised, half-breed Samaritans was traveling on that road, and he came to where the beaten, half-dead man was. When the Samaritan saw the beaten man's desperate condition, his compassion for the man moved him to act. ³⁴The Samaritan went over to the beaten, half-dead man and administered first aid to him by disinfecting and bandaging his wounds. Then, the Samaritan man set the beaten man on the Samaritan's donkey and took him to an inn where he could take better care of him. ³⁵The next day, the Samaritan took out two silver coins to pay the innkeeper and said, 'Take care of this man. This should be enough money to cover this man's lodging for two days. However, if it ends up costing more to help him, then put it in on my bill. I will repay you for any extra expenses you incur when I return.'

³⁶"Now, from this story, let Me ask you—which of these three people do you think was being a neighbor as God intends to the man beaten by robbers?"

³⁷The expert in the Jewish law replied, "The one who showed mercy to him."

Then Jesus responded, "Exactly! There is no need to worry about who your neighbor is because everyone is your neighbor. Now go and love all people, serving their needs regardless of who they are."

### 5.2.2. Following Christ requires a balanced life of faith (10:38–42).

³⁸As Jesus and His disciples continued their journey toward Jerusalem, they entered a village and were welcomed into the home of a woman named Martha. ³⁹Martha had a sister named Mary, who, during His visit, sat at the Lord's feet the entire time listening to His teaching. ⁴⁰But Martha was overwhelmed with all the work that went into preparing such a large meal for all her guests. As preparations for the event continued, she approached Jesus and asked, "Surely it bothers You that my sister has left me to do all this work by myself, that she just sits there instead of helping? Please tell her to come in and help me."

⁴¹The Lord answered her, "My dear Martha, I understand that you are anxious and distressed about many things, ⁴²but do not be so worried about all the things you have to do that you lose focus of the most important thing of all. Sometimes tasks and services need to be suspended in order to maintain the relationship necessary to and to learn from God's teaching. In this case, Mary has focused on the most important thing, and it will not be taken away from her."

### 5.2.3. *Following Christ requires a healthy life of prayer (11:1–13).*

## CHAPTER 11

¹One day, Jesus was praying in a particular place. When He finished praying, one of His disciples approached Him and said, "Lord, John the Baptist taught his disciples to pray. Will You teach us how to pray?"

²Then Jesus gave them this guidance: "When you pray together, here is a model to follow. Pray like this:

"Loving Father,
May Your holy and unique character be honored, admired, and respected.
May Your kingdom rule and reign come in the fullness of Your power and be experienced among us now while we wait for its arrival.
³As we go through life, we recognize that You are the provider for our most basic needs, even our food, and we trust in Your daily provision.

⁴And forgive us of our sins and shortcomings
>to the extent that we forgive those who sin and miss the mark with us.

As we are faced with temptation, deliver us from it by giving us the power to resist it."

⁵Then Jesus instructed them on how they should approach God in prayer, saying, "Imagine the following situation: it is midnight and a friend shows up needing your hospitality, but you are out of food. Not wanting to be inhospitable at this late hour, you go over to your next-door neighbor's house and say, 'Friend, can you lend me three loaves of bread? ⁶I have had a friend arrive tonight that we were not expecting till tomorrow. They are hungry, and all the bread we baked earlier today is gone. I am out of food for the night and have nothing to offer them. Can you help me be a good host and let me have some bread to provide for them?' ⁷Obviously, the natural response from the next-door neighbor would be, 'Please do not disturb my family and me at this late hour. We have already locked the doors on our one-bedroom house, and my children are in bed for the night. I cannot get up, disturbing everyone else in the house, and help you tonight.' ⁸But here is the point: your neighbor will not disturb his family, get up, and give you what you need just because you are friends. He will put your request off until tomorrow. However, if you remain bold, persistent, and keep shamelessly knocking—to the point that it wakes up everyone anyway—then your neighbor will get up and give you whatever you need.

⁹"So I say to you, learn a lesson from this story. When you approach God in prayer, come to Him boldly, persistently, and shamelessly. Ask and you will receive what you ask for. Seek and you will find what you are looking for. Knock and the door will be opened to you. ¹⁰You see, unlike a reluctant neighbor woken in the middle of the night, God always stands ready to hear from you and to meet your needs. He wants to give you good things, wants to help you find what you need, and wants to open the door to you. So, in prayer, approach Him boldly, persistently, and shamelessly. For everyone who asks receives. Everyone who seeks finds. Everyone who knocks will have the door opened.

¹¹"And do not think you are bugging God when you pray in this bold, persistent manner. To gain a better appreciation for God's nature toward His children and how you are not bugging Him, let us look at the dynamic of a good, human Father with his son. If a child came to his father and asked for a fish, how many good fathers do you know who would give their child a snake instead? ¹²Or, if the child came asking for an egg, how many good fathers do you know who would give their child a poisonous spider instead? ¹³So, if a good father—one who is still an imperfect human prone to sin and missing the mark—knows how to be good to their children and give them what they ask for and need, how much more do you think your loving, Heavenly Father will give the Holy Spirit to those who ask Him!"

### 5.3. The life of following Christ calls for one to trust in His authority, His truth, and the light of His teaching (11:14–54).

#### 5.3.1. Following Christ calls for one to trust in Jesus' power and authority (11:14–23).

¹⁴One day, Jesus was casting out a demon who had made a man mute. When the demon had been cast out, the man was able to speak again. The crowd marveled at the miracle, ¹⁵but some in the crowd debated where Jesus' power and authority came from. Some people claimed, "He must be an agent of Beelzebul"—another name for Satan, the prince of demons—"He must be casting demons out through demonic power." ¹⁶Others did not suspect demonic power, but they were not yet convinced it was God's power either. These people were skeptical, and they kept testing Jesus, looking for some kind of extraordinary, spectacular miracle or ever elusive piece of evidence that would somehow definitely meet their standards and prove things to them.

¹⁷Jesus knew their thoughts and addressed them by saying, "Any kingdom divided in a perpetual civil war is doomed. A family constantly fighting with each other will break apart. ¹⁸You claim that Satan's power is at work in Me, but how is that even possible? Why would Satan, who longs to destroy what he can, be actively working to heal things through Me? If Satan's kingdom constantly fights against itself like this, how can it possibly survive? It makes no sense for Satan to fight against himself. ¹⁹Also, if I am casting out demons by Beelzebul's

(Satan's) power, what about your Jewish sons—My followers from Jewish backgrounds—who are casting out demons? Are they agents of Satan working under his power and influence too? No, they are not working by Satan's power. Instead, they have been empowered with an authority that will allow them to one day serve as your judges, if you do not have a change of heart. [20]And here is the truth you must reckon with: if I am not casting out demons by Satan's power, there is only one other option: it is God's power at work in Me. If I am casting out demons through the powerful finger of God's mighty touch, then the kingdom of God—the power of His rule and reign—has now come and arrived among you.

[21]"You see, there is a cosmic, spiritual battle over who rules going on right here, right now. There is a strong man—Satan—who is fully armed with guards stationed around the perimeter of his house, who is trying to keep his possessions safe inside. [22]However, when One who has superior strength attacks and overpowers him, the Stronger Man is able to strip and take away Satan's armor (which he depended on) and divide up all his goods as the victorious spoils of war.

[23]"In the end, there are only two sides to this cosmic, spiritual battle, and you must choose your side. Whoever is not with Me is My enemy, and whoever is not working with Me is actually working against Me.

> 5.3.2. Following Christ calls for one to make a decisive decision to trust in Him and the light of His teaching (11:24–36).

[24]"Keep in mind that this spiritual battle involves your life and requires you to make crucial choices. For example, consider this dangerous illustration of someone who was initially freed by God's grace but then refused to continue to live by His grace. When an evil spirit is exorcised from a person, it wanders around. Like traveling in a dry, arid land, it ventures around trying to find a hospitable place to rest and does not find it. Not finding a place to rest, it returns to the person it was cast out from. It says, 'I will go back and try that person's house again.' [25]When the evil spirit arrives, it finds that the spiritual house has been cleaned out—swept clean, totally in order, but also totally empty inside. [26]However, with the door left wide open and a completely empty spiritual space ready for habitation, the demon

goes inside. Since the spiritual house is completely empty from being cleaned out, the evil spirit brings with him seven other spirits that are even more wicked than itself. They all go into the person's house and live there. Since the person only responded to God's grace temporarily, long enough to clean out the evil presence from their lives, but did not choose to live continually in God's grace, that person left the door of their spiritual house wide open for evil to return. And it did. Since that person remained spiritually neutral and did not continue to respond to God, in the end, their spiritual situation is even worse than it was before the first demon was cast out."

[27] As Jesus was saying these things, a woman in the crowd was impressed with His wisdom. She wanted to honor Him. So she did what was customary in that time and gave honor to the mother that brought Jesus into the world. She said, "May God show special favor on the mother who gave birth to You and raised You."

[28] Jesus, taking the opportunity to highlight those who are really blessed by God in life, replied, "Those who enjoy God's special favor—His richness and the fullness of life He gives—are not those who share a biological or social origin. Instead, those who enjoy God's special favor in life are those who hear God's Word and obey it, putting His Word into practice in their daily lives."

[29] As Jesus continued to teach, the crowd just kept getting bigger as more people came to hear Him. Sensing that these people were just looking for the latest bit of spiritual insight to consume, Jesus said, "What an incredibly misguided and wicked generation this is. It constantly searches for the newest or trendiest nugget of knowledge or the next miraculous achievement to guide it. It is not interested in real or lasting change; it does not seek to continually walk the path that leads to true life. This misguided generation seeks something it considers definitive or miraculous to prove the truth, but nothing will be given to it except the same sign that Jonah gave his generation: the message of God's truth and teaching.

[30] "Just as Jonah was God's messenger of truth to his generation, so also will the Son of Man be God's messenger of truth to this generation. [31] Back during the times of King Solomon, as mentioned in 1

Kings 10:1-13, the most powerful Queen of that time—the Queen of the South—traveled many miles to hear Solomon's wisdom. She did not have the full truth of God as this generation does today, yet she responded to the knowledge she had at that time. At the judgment, the Queen of the South and the faithful will rise in judgment of today's generation. They will condemn it for not responding to God's message of truth. She will judge them because she did not need some miraculous sign to trust God but responded in faith to the limited portion of God's revelation she heard from Solomon, who was the wisest man the earth has ever known. And the saddest thing about this current generation is that it has received the full revelation of God's truth from One who is far greater than Solomon, but they refuse to respond to it.

$^{32}$"Likewise, the men of Nineveh who heard Jonah's teaching will also stand up at the judgment of this generation and condemn it. Why? Because they were faithful and responded to Jonah's message and the limited portion of God's revelation they received at that time. However, this current generation has received One far greater than Jonah, One who has given them the full revelation of God's truth, but they refuse to respond to it.

$^{33}$"God has not hidden His truth from anyone. No one lights a candle, bringing light to the darkness, and then puts it in a place or in a box where its light will be hidden; neither does God. Instead, One who brings light to the darkness puts it on a stand so that everyone may see and benefit from the light. $^{34}$God's light has been lit, but your eye must receive His light. Your eye is the gatekeeper that allows light to enter your body or not. When your eye is good, it lets God's light in, and then your entire body is full of His light. But when your eye is bad, it shuts God's light out, and then your whole body is full of darkness.

$^{35}$"In the end, the crucial choice is yours. See to it, then, that your life is full of light and not darkness. $^{36}$God's light is shining down on your life like the sun. If you let God's light in, the darkness that was with you will be replaced by light, and the darkness will disappear. If you let God's light in, your entire life will be filled with a divine, spiritual light that will perpetually shine from within you."

> *5.3.3. Following Christ calls for one to trust in His truth with a heart that is not blind or hard to His teaching (11:37–54).*

[37]When Jesus had finished speaking, a Pharisee invited Him to dinner. Jesus went to his house, reclined at his table, and ate with him. [38]The Pharisees were shocked when Jesus did not follow their custom and ate without ceremonially washing His hands first.

[39]Realizing their legalistic judgment, the Lord said to him, "Let us shed light on the darkness of your perspective. You Pharisees focus on making sure the outside of your cup and dish are clean. However, you do not pay attention to how dirty the inside of the cup is; you do not recognize that it is actually full of greed and wickedness.

[40]"You are foolish for just focusing on cleaning the outside and overlooking all that is on the inside. Surely you know that the One who made the outside made the inside too? [41]Let us examine what is on the inside for a second. If the light of God's truth were in you, your heart would be motivated to be generous to the poor. Then the cleanliness you like to present on the outside would be matched by a real cleanliness on the inside.

[42]"How pitiful and unfortunate you are in God's eyes because you tithe a tenth of all your money, produce, and whatever else you have, yet you neglect justice and the love of God for those in need. Outwardly, you tithe as though you have been changed by God, but inwardly you are motivated to do nothing to help those who are carrying a heavy load through this life. You should have practiced consideration for the poor and had compassion on them instead of patting yourselves on the back for what you tithe. One reflects an inward and outward cleanliness of the heart; the other does not.

[43]"How pitiful and unfortunate you are in God's eyes because, in pride, you love the most important seats in the religious assembly; you revel in pride when others look up to you in public because of your religious position.

[44]"How pitiful and unfortunate you are in God's eyes because you are an unrecognized presence of death to others. Like unmarked graves

that people walk over without knowing death is beneath them, you lead people into ways of spiritual death without them knowing it."

⁴⁵Upon hearing these rebukes, an expert in the religious law interjected, "Teacher, when You say such strong things to the Pharisees, do You realize how much You are insulting us too?"

⁴⁶Jesus replied, "Oh, do not think I do not have some words directed for you too. How pitiful and unfortunate you experts in the religious law are in God's eyes because you put heavy religious regulations and guidelines on the people. You have so legalistically burdened their religious practice that they can hardly carry the heavy loads you have put upon them. Worse, you hypocrites will do nothing, not even lift one finger, to help those people who are trying to follow your burdensome teaching.

⁴⁷"How pitiful and unfortunate you are in God's eyes because you carry on a tradition that neglects to respond to God's message when it is presented. ⁴⁸Just like your spiritual forefathers who killed the prophets of the past, you also build tombs for God's prophets. In doing so, you do not honor God's message delivered through those prophets. Instead, you honor yourselves; you elevate yourselves above God as though you get to judge what God has or has not said through His prophets. You even take pride in not responding to God's message by dismissing it as not from Him when you do not agree with what He has said. ⁴⁹You fail to recognize that God sends you His wisdom in the time of His choosing through His prophets. It is to your eternal detriment not to respond to God's revelation. He even told you that He will send you His message in Jeremiah 7:25, where He said, 'I will send them prophets and apostles to deliver My message to them, some of whom they will kill and others they will just persecute.' Yet you do not listen to God's message revealed to you.

⁵⁰"Make no mistake: this generation will not escape responsibility before God, no matter how hard it tries to avoid it. When you do not respond to God's message, you will be held responsible for the blood of all the martyred prophets that has been shed since the beginning of the world. By rejecting and not responding to God's message in the present, you are no different than those who rejected His truth in the

past. ⁵¹From the first blood that was shed on the earth when Abel was murdered to Zechariah, the last, recognized Jewish prophet who was killed between the ark and the sanctuary, you will be held responsible. You, just like your spiritual forefathers, will be held accountable for the killing, persecuting, and rejection of God's messengers.

⁵²"How pitiful and unfortunate are you experts in religious law in God's eyes because you have taken away the key to proper religious knowledge and understanding. You have refused to receive God's message for yourselves, and by doing so, you hinder and misdirect those who are trying to seek God."

⁵³When Jesus left the dinner after finishing what He was saying, the Pharisees and the experts of the religious law began to oppose Him fiercely. They began to press Jesus hard by questioning everything He said. ⁵⁴Like predators lying in wait, they sought to catch Jesus in some serious error so that they might be able to get rid of Him for good.

### 5.4. The life of following Christ requires a faithful pursuit of trusting in and serving Him with an undistracted eye (12:1–48).

#### 5.4.1. Following Christ calls one to fear harming God's reputation in the world more than fearing what others think (12:1–12).

#### CHAPTER 12

¹In the meantime, the crowds grew around Jesus and His followers. Several thousand people were now gathered around them. It was so crowded that people were trampling upon one another. Seeing their growing popularity among the people, Jesus taught His hearers it was more important to honor and respect God—to fear Him—than to focus honor and respect on other people and what they think—to fear any human being. Jesus made this point by saying to them, "Be on your guard against the false teachings of the Pharisees. Even just giving in to a little bit of their misdirected teaching can be like yeast that spreads and permeates through the entire batch of dough. ²You can try to keep your inner, true self hidden from others. But you fail to realize that you cannot hide behind a mask and fool God. Before

God, everything that has been covered up will be exposed and seen for what it is. ³Whatever you have spoken in the darkness will be heard in the light; whatever you have whispered behind closed doors—the stuff you thought you could hide from the world—will be shouted out from the rooftops. You cannot hide from God.

⁴"So who should you fear more? Should you worry more about what people can do to you, or should you worry more about what God can do to you? My friends, let Me tell you this truth: do not be afraid of those who can only kill your physical body. They cannot do any more harm to you after you are physically dead. ⁵Instead, you should fear God, giving all your honor and respect to the One who has the power not only to kill you physically but who also has the power and authority to throw your entire being into hell. Without a doubt, He is the One you should truly be concerned about!

⁶"Fear God, making Him the focus of your life and giving Him all your honor and respect, and you will have nothing else to worry about. For example, think about small birds such as sparrows. You can buy a few of them for just some loose change, right? Yet not a single one of these sparrows—these small birds—is forgotten by God; He takes care of them all. ⁷And do you not realize that you are more valuable to God than millions upon millions of sparrows? For example, God cares for you so much that He even knows the exact number of hairs on your head at this very moment. Do you think someone who knows you so intimately and completely will not care for you? He does and will!

⁸"I tell you this truth: everyone who openly and freely acknowledges Me, the Son of Man, before others will also freely and openly acknowledge in the presence of God's angels. ⁹But whoever is afraid to be affiliated with Me and denies Me before others will not be affiliated with Me; I will deny knowing them in the presence of God's angels. ¹⁰Anyone can have a bad moment; anyone can have instances when they say something bad about Me or stand against Me and still be forgiven. However, anyone who makes a prolonged, continual habit of rejecting the Holy Spirit's truth to them and speaks against Him consistently will not be forgiven; they will experience a permanent rejection by God.

¹¹"And when the day of persecution comes, when you are brought to stand trial before the religious leaders in front of the religious assembly, do not worry about how to defend your position of faith or what you will say, ¹²for the Holy Spirit will give you the right words to say when the time comes."

> 5.4.2. Following Christ calls one to take a proper perspective toward resources (12:13–21).

¹³Then someone in the crowd said to Jesus, "Teacher, please take my side in a dispute with my brother and tell him to divide our family's inheritance with me. I want it."

¹⁴Jesus replied, "Friend, what makes you think I am like your other religious leaders and will step in to serve as an umpire who settles your disputes?" ¹⁵Then Jesus expanded on the real issue and said, "You should always be on constant guard against all different types of greed and the selfish attitude that consumes one who is focused on wealth. After all, life is not measured by how much wealth you have or by what you can get for yourself."

¹⁶Then Jesus told them a parable: "The farm of a rich man produced an abundant crop one year. ¹⁷He thought to himself, 'What shall I do? I have nowhere to store up all of my crops. I have to do something now, even if it means neglecting everything else so that I can benefit from all this wealth.'

¹⁸"Then the rich man said, 'I know what I'll do! I'll tear down my little barns and build bigger ones right over the top of them. Then I'll have enough space to store all the surplus grain. ¹⁹And I will proudly say to myself, "Now you have enough goods stored up to last you for many years. You do not have to worry about anyone or anything else anymore. Just focus on doing whatever makes you happy. As the cultural proverb says, 'Eat, drink, and be merry.'"'

²⁰"But then God said to this man, 'You have been such a fool with your selfish, greedy attitude of just focusing on whatever you can get. You will die this very night, and then what will become of everything you

selfishly worked so hard to gain for yourself?'

²¹"This outcome is what awaits anyone who becomes self-centered and self-destructive in their attitude toward gaining wealth, for anyone who seeks out riches merely for his or her own selfish gain instead of focusing on what matters most—having an attitude that values becoming rich in one's relationship with God more than any other type of wealth."

> 5.4.3. *Following Christ calls one not to worry but to trust in God's provision for one's life (12:22–34).*

²²Then Jesus turned to His disciples and continued, "In light of what was just said about the danger of one's attitude toward what they have, I want you to learn to trust God with everything. Do not be anxious and worry about your life—what you will eat, about your body, or what you will wear. ²³For your inner life and spiritual wellbeing are more important than any food you put into your body, and there is more to your outer appearance than the clothes that hang on your body. ²⁴Look at and consider the ravens. They are considered the lowliest and most scavenger-like of all the birds. They do not plant any seed, nor do they reap a harvest or store up their goods in a barn. However, God provides for their needs and feeds them. And you are considerably more valuable to God than any birds! ²⁵Is there anyone who can add a single hour to their life by worrying about it? ²⁶No! So if you cannot do this one little thing—extending your life by one hour through worry—then why in the world should you be worried about all the bigger things in your life that are beyond your control?

²⁷"You should think about the lilies in the field and carefully consider how they grow. There is not one ounce of labor or worry in their existence. Yet, as they simply do what they were created to do, they are adorned with more splendor and wonder than Solomon, the richest and wisest person who ever lived. ²⁸If God cares that much about the flowers of the field, which are here today and thrown into the fire tomorrow, then how much more do you think He will care for you? Oh, you people of little faith, do not cast doubts on God's care for you!

²⁹"Do not focus your mind and heart on what you will eat or what you

will drink. Do not be so worried and preoccupied with these things that you miss out on what God is giving you. ³⁰For the people who do not know God chase after these things. However, as a person who knows God, you should not chase after these things because you know you have a Father who already knows about your needs. ³¹Instead of worrying about your life and its concerns, you seek His kingdom by constantly focusing on living life as a representative of God's rule and government. As you live life guided by His rule, you can trust that God will take care of you.

³²"So do not be afraid. Even though you are like a little flock of sheep prone to worry and fright, you have a Father who is a caring Shepherd. He thoroughly enjoys taking care of His own and giving those under His leadership what they need. ³³If you are living a life focused on being a representative of God's rule and government, then you are freed from worrying about life and can be generous with what God has given you. You can sell your possessions and give to those in need. A life lived like this generates wealth in a heavenly bank, a bank in the place where God is that will never be robbed, will never fail, and will never be destroyed. ³⁴To determine if you have the right focus in life, you should ask yourself one question: are you building up your wealth in God's heavenly bank or not? For wherever you are building up your treasure, that is where your heart and true values will also be.

> 5.4.4. *Following Christ calls one to be a faithful steward with the resources He has provided (12:35–48).*

³⁵"To store up treasure in heaven, you must always be prepared and ready to serve God. Like wearing a shirt, you must constantly be dressed and ready to go out in it. Like a light that shines through the darkness, you must keep God's light in you turned on all night long. ³⁶Be always ready like servants who are waiting for their master to return from a big wedding celebration. They do not know when their master will return from the wedding party. So they make sure that when he arrives and knocks on the door, they will be ready to open the door to him. ³⁷And what do you think the results will be for those servants who have been faithful? The servants who are ready and watching for his return will be especially favored in God's sight. I tell

you this amazing truth: in an astonishing reversal of roles, the Master will be so pleased with His faithful servants that He will continuously serve them. His service to His faithful servants will be so joyful that it will be like they are partaking in a great wedding feast together.

[38]"It does not matter when the master comes. If he comes in the middle of the night or just before daybreak, the servants who are constantly ready for his arrival will be the ones especially favored in God's sight. [39]You need to understand this dynamic of continual, faithful service, so let Me say it another way. If a homeowner knew exactly when a thief was coming, he would not have stayed out and let his home be robbed. He would have been ready for the thief at that time. [40]But you are not going to know when He will come. So, you must constantly be prepared and be ready, because you will never know when the Son of Man will arrive. Like a thief in the night, He will come at a time when you do not expect Him."

[41]Looking to clarify, Peter asked: "Lord, who is responsible for following this teaching of being a faithful servant always ready to serve? Is this teaching just for the twelve apostles, or is it for every one of Your followers?"

[42]The Lord replied, "Asking about whose responsibility it is to be a servant avoids the main principle. The main point is everyone should focus on being a faithful servant. Let Me illustrate this point further. A faithful and wise servant is one whom the master can put in charge of managing his staff and who will ensure they eat on time. [43]If the master returns and finds that his manager has done a good job, then that faithful servant will be favored in the master's eyes. [44]The truth of this situation is that the master will be so pleased with his faithful and trustworthy servant that he will put his servant in charge of everything he owns. [45]But let us consider what would happen if the servant is not faithful in his service. What will happen if a servant says, 'My master is likely not coming back any time soon, and I have got a while before he does,' and then the servant begins to abuse all the other staff, both men and women, and decides just to party, stuff his face, and get drunk? [46]Even though the unfaithful servant is living that way, one day, the master of the servant will return at an unannounced and unexpected time. The master will discover what his unfaithful servant

has done, and he will cut his unfaithful servant into pieces, rejecting his very existence by throwing the unfaithful servant into the pit assigned to the unbelievers.

⁴⁷"There is no way around it: a servant who knows what the master wants but ignores it and does not prepare or get ready for it will be severely punished with strong disciplinary action. ⁴⁸However, a servant who does not know what the mater wants and yet does the things deserving of punishment will only receive a light punishment. Do you see the difference between the faithful and unfaithful servant—how the person who knows God's grace should be focused on the kind of service he or she can offer to God, and how everyone is responsible to God to serve Him from what they have been given? For from everyone who has been given much, much will be demanded; and from the one entrusted with much, much more will be required.

### 5.5. The life of following Christ requires recognizing the nature and limitations of time (12:49–14:24).

#### 5.5.1. Following Christ calls one to recognize that following Him can cause one to be divided from those who reject Him (12:49–13:9).

##### 5.5.1.a. Be ready to encounter division when following Christ (12:49-53).

⁴⁹"Do not be fooled about why I am here. I have come to start a fire on the earth, a spiritual work that will make decisive judgments and purge all sin and wickedness from it. Oh, how I wish these purifying flames were already burning! ⁵⁰But I am constrained right now. I must first undergo a terrible baptism of suffering, experiencing the judgment of sin on others' behalf so that they will have the opportunity to be spared from it. Once this terrible baptism of suffering has been accomplished, the price will be paid, and I will be free from the heavy burden I must face.

⁵¹"Do not be fooled about why I am here and what that means. Do you think I came to earth only to bring peace to it? If you believe that, you

are sadly mistaken. Let Me tell you why I am here. I am here to force you to make hard choices about your relationship with God. I have not come to create a warm and fuzzy peace for all people but to divide those who choose to follow God from those who do not. ⁵²From now on, even people who belong to the same family will be divided from one another because some decided to follow Me. For example, in a family of five, there will either be a majority who choose to follow Me and a minority who do not. Or it could be the opposite. ⁵³Either way, I am here to force a choice—you either follow Me or you do not. And how individuals in a family respond to Me will cause divisions in the family. A father may be divided against his son or a son set against his father. A mother may be divided against her daughter or a daughter set against her mother. A mother-in-law may be divided against her daughter-in-law or a daughter-in-law set against her mother-in-law."

> 5.5.1.b. Be ready and able to discern what God is doing and how He is working in the world (12:54-59).

⁵⁴Then Jesus turned to the crowd and said, "Are you not capable of discerning the present reality before you and what it means? When you see a cloud beginning to roll in from the west, what do you say? You say, 'It is going to rain,' and you are right. ⁵⁵When the wind blows southwest, bringing heat from the desert, what do you say? You say, 'It is going to be scorching hot,' and your perception is right. ⁵⁶But you bunch of pretending, fraudulent hypocrites! You can discern the natural change in weather by looking at the earth and sky, but you cannot tell the supernatural change that is happening right in front of your faces right now! How can you miss all that I am doing around you at this present time?

> 5.5.1.c. Be ready to settle accounts before God (12:57-59).

⁵⁷"You do not have to be a genius to figure these things out. The simple truth is right in front of you. Why can you not make the right decision about it? ⁵⁸But you must recognize that your decision about Me will determine how you will settle your relationship with God. Let Me illustrate this point. Imagine you owe a significant debt to an accuser, and they are threatening to take you to court over it. You should try to settle the matter before going to court, right? Otherwise, when your accuser lets the judge know just how severe your debt is, the judge will

pass a severe penalty on you. The judge will turn you over to the officer who will throw you in prison. ⁵⁹And debtor's prison is not a pleasant place; in debtor's prison, inmates are beaten severely and not released until the last penny of their debt has been paid. Likewise, the debt on your account before God is serious business. You need to settle your debt with Him before you face His judgment.

    5.5.1.d.   Be ready because life will end for all eventually (13:1-9).

## CHAPTER 13

¹Around this time, there were some present who relayed some scandalous news to Jesus. They told Him about the people from Galilee who had been massacred and whose blood Pilate had intentionally mixed with the blood of the Temple sacrifices. ²Considering it was a severe disgrace to have the blood of those massacred mixed with animal's blood, Jesus knew His listeners would default to blaming the people from Galilee who were massacred; they would assume there must have tremendous sin in their lives that caused such a terrible disgrace. Knowing what they were thinking, Jesus addressed the issue with them. He said, "Do you think all of those Galileans who were massacred are worse sinners than all the other people in Galilee? Do you think they suffered such terrible disgrace because they had more sin than you? ³No, that is not the case at all! Those people who suffered tragedy are no different in their sin than you are. You need to realize that you are sinners, too, and that while you may not suffer such a terrible disgrace in death as they did, your life will end; death will come to you in one form or another. Unless you repent—changing the way you think and live toward God, which will change the direction and eternal fate of your life—you will perish in your sin and be lost eternally.

⁴"And what do you think about the other tragic news we have heard about the eighteen people who died when an earthquake caused the tower of Siloam to fall on them? Do you think that since they died in a terrible and tragic natural disaster, they must have been the worst sinners in Jerusalem? ⁵Let Me tell you the reality very plainly: no, that is not the case. A natural disaster did not kill them as a form of punishment from God. God did not punish them because they were worse sinners than you are. They were nothing more than sinners just as

you are. Whether by a terrible and tragic natural disaster or by other means, their lives were going to end, just as yours will someday. So, do not focus on the gossipy speculation about whether the severity of one's sin leads to divine punishment; instead, focus on the fact that all people are sinners and will die. Realize that you are a sinner and that everyone will die physically one day. Recognizing these realities, you should repent—changing the way you think and live toward God, which will change the direction and eternal fate of your life. If you do not repent and turn toward God, then you will die spiritually, too, and eternally perish."

[6]Then Jesus shared with them a story with a significant spiritual point, a story that used the imagery of a vineyard—often associated with the nation of Israel—and a fig tree to describe the people's collective negative response to God's message. Jesus said, "There was a man who had a fig tree planted in his vineyard. One day, he came back looking to see if any fruit had grown on it. But he did not find any. [7]Then he said to the gardener of the vineyard, 'Why has this fig tree not produced any fruit? For three years, I have been coming to look at it to see if it has produced any fruit, and I have not found any. My patience has worn thin. Why let this unresponsive tree use up the good soil? It is time to cut it down!'

[8]"But the gardener replied, 'Sir, let us give it one more chance, one more year. I will give it special attention and fertilize it. [9]Maybe this unresponsive tree will finally respond and produce fruit in the next year. If it does, great! But if it does not respond within the limited time you have given to it, then you can cut it down.'"

> 5.5.2. *Following Christ calls one to be faithful, while others refuse to respond to Him (13:10-17).*

[10]One Sabbath, Jesus was teaching in the Jewish synagogue, their place dedicated to worship. [11]While teaching, Jesus saw a woman there who had been physically crippled by an evil spirit for over eighteen years. She was bent over and unable to stand straight up at all. [12]When Jesus saw her, He was moved with compassion and called to her: "Dear woman, you have endured so much physical suffering and spiritual antagonism for all these years. But right now, I am going to heal you,

setting you free from your sickness." ¹³Then Jesus laid His hands on her, conveying His healing power to her through His touch. Immediately, she was able to stand up straight. She recognized what had happened and who had done it, thanking and praising God for her healing.

¹⁴Upon seeing what Jesus had done, and because it was the Sabbath, the religious leader of the Jewish synagogue responded by saying to the people, "According to the teaching in Exodus 20:9-10, six days of the week are allowed for work. The Jewish traditions collected in the Mishnah that seek to expand this scriptural teaching defines what can and cannot be done on the Sabbath before one breaks the Sabbath commandment. While I am not exactly sure which of those prohibitions applies here, I am sure one of them was just broken. And you should not break the Jewish tradition of what is allowed on the Sabbath. Instead of breaking the Sabbath law, you should come back and be healed on one of the other six days in the week; do not do it on the Sabbath."

¹⁵Jesus replied: "You religious leaders are such hypocrites! You are saying it is more important to keep the legalistic 'tradition' around the commandment than to have compassion for a person who is in physical and spiritual need? Do you not realize that every Sabbath, when you untie your ox or your donkey from the stall and lead it to water, you are breaking the legalistic 'tradition' that says you cannot walk more than three thousand feet on the Sabbath? ¹⁶You do not frown upon breaking your Sabbath tradition to meet the needs of your animals. Yet here is a daughter of Abraham (a fellow Jewish person like you), whom Satan has held in bondage for eighteen years! Considering how much compassion you show toward meeting the needs of your animals, should you not show even more compassion on meeting the physical and spiritual needs of this woman?"

¹⁷After Jesus had said this, all of His opponents were humiliated and put to shame. The rest of the people rejoiced at all the wonderful things Jesus was doing.

> 5.5.3. *Following Christ calls one to faithfully focus on His kingdom's coming while others may choose another path in life, which will lead to their own peril (13:18–35).*
>
>> 5.5.3.a. God's kingdom is growing in this world and will continue to grow gradually into greatness, eventually covering the entire earth (13:18-21).

¹⁸Then Jesus said, "How can I get you all to understand how God's rule is working in the world now and how He will bring it to complete fulfillment later? Let Me further illustrate how God's kingdom will come about. ¹⁹God's kingdom at work in this world is like a mustard seed (or pine nut) that a man planted in his garden. Inevitably and over time, what appears to be a small, insignificant seed grows to become a huge, incredibly significant tree that is so large birds find shelter and make their nests in its branches."

²⁰Jesus continued, "How about I give you another picture of how God's kingdom will not come all at once, and how it will not come about through some cultural overhaul or through political or military might? ²¹God's kingdom at work in this world is like a small pinch of yeast that a woman used in a large amount of bread she was making for a huge party. She mixed that small pinch of yeast into over sixty pounds of flour. Yet when that small pinch of yeast had been mixed in, it worked its way through and completely permeated the entire batch of dough."

>> 5.5.3.b. God's kingdom is coming, and people should respond now, before the door of opportunity closes (13:22-30).

²²As Jesus was pressing on in His journey toward Jerusalem, Jesus went through various towns and villages. He taught others as he traveled along. ²³One person who was listening to Him was somewhat perceptive, and said, "Lord, Your teaching seems to limit salvation, implying that one's nationality and heritage may not be enough. Are there only a few of the faithful people who are going to be saved?"

Jesus replied, ²⁴"To ask how many are going to be saved is the wrong question. The right question is this: are you going to be saved? You should focus your mind on your life with God. If you are going to be part of God's kingdom, the space where His rule and peace are active, then you must give your total attention to it. You must strive to enter by the specific route—the narrow door—that brings you under His rule and into His kingdom. I am telling you, there will be many who will try to enter His kingdom on their own, self-made, self-reasoned, or self-justified paths, but they will not be able to enter. There will be many who seek to enter by these routes or other alternative paths not designed by God, but they will not be able to enter His kingdom because they did not choose the path God revealed to them.

25"And the time to choose God's path—the narrow door He has provided—is running out! There will come a time when the master of the house gets up and locks the door. When that happens, it will be too late to enter God's house. You will stand outside, knocking and pleading, 'Lord, open the door for us!'

"But He will reply, 'Sorry, I do not know you or where you come from.'

26"Then you will try to bargain your way in by saying, 'But we have been around a long time, hung out with You in the past, and have been in Your presence. In the past, we ate and drank with You. We have even heard Your teaching before.'

27"But the Master will reply, 'Outward knowledge about Me or some kind of loose association with Me is not enough. No matter how much you may disagree, you do not get to choose your own path to enter into My kingdom. I provided you a path, but you did not use it. I provided you with a door—the kind of door that opens and develops a deep, personal knowledge of Me—but you chose not to enter through it. I am sorry, but you do not know the first thing about Me. The party in My house is only for the people I have a relationship with, for those who have been living rightly with God. So, all those who failed to respond when you had a chance, depart from Me and leave this place. You do not belong here. In My sight, you are the same as any other wicked evildoer.'

28"What will be the end result for these people, the people who are on the outside looking in on the party at God's house? Their eyes will be filled with tears, and they will be filled with so much frustration that their teeth will grind. They will see their spiritual forefathers, the people they heard all the past stories about—people such as Abraham, Isaac, Jacob, and all the Old Testament prophets—living joyfully inside God's kingdom. But you who did not respond will just be on the outside looking in; you will have no place there. ²⁹You will watch all kinds of people you considered religious outsiders and those you considered unworthy because of their background stream in from all over the world. From the east, west, north, and south, they will come from all over the world and enjoy the party inside God's house. Why? Because they have walked the specific route God provided and have entered God's house through the narrow door. As a result, they will take their rightful place inside God's kingdom and join in with everyone else at God's party. ³⁰Pay special attention to this simple reality: some who have the least amount of spiritual privilege and religious opportunity but who responded faithfully to Me will have the most and be celebrated at the party. However, the opposite is also true. Those who have the greatest amount of spiritual privilege and religious opportunity will receive the least because they do not respond to Me, and they will not be able to join the party."

> 5.5.3.c. God's kingdom is coming, and those who do not respond to Jesus will not only miss it but seal their fate (13:31-35).

³¹Just as Jesus was finishing His teaching, some Pharisees came to Him under a manipulative guise of goodwill. They said, "Oh my, you have caught the attention of the Roman Governor of our region, Herod Antipas. We have heard he wants to kill You! You should run; leave this place and go somewhere else to protect Yourself!"

³²Jesus replied, "I will not be deterred from My mission by anyone. You can go tell that sly and crafty fox and anyone like him that 'For a period of time called "today and tomorrow," I will do the work God gave Me to do—the work of casting out demons, healing people, and accomplishing My purpose on the time period called the 'third day' when I will have reached My goal.' ³³But achieving My goal on the third day comes later. For right now, it is still the period of time called 'today and tomorrow.' In these days, I must continue on My way forward and toward My final destination. After all, it would never do for a prophet of God to be killed anywhere but in Jerusalem!

³⁴"Oh Jerusalem, Jerusalem! You have had a front-row seat to God's chosen messengers, yet you killed the prophets and stoned those God sent to you. I have yearned with great desire to gather all your children together just as a hen gathers her chicks together under her wing. But you would not listen; you have not responded or let Me! ³⁵And now it is too late. You had your opportunity. You did not respond to God's truth when you had the chance. So now you will be left all alone. The area where you live will be forsaken and abandoned. You will not see Me approach you again until you see Me arriving as a powerful, mighty, heavenly King in the fullness of God's glory. At that time, you will recognize My Kingly status and My rule over all things, and you will realize that I fulfill the truth in the words of Psalm 118:26 that say, 'May continual favor and joy rest on He who comes in the name of the Lord and brings His rule.'"

> 5.5.4. Following Christ calls for living a life of humble faithfulness while others may or may not respond to God's work (14:1–24).

## CHAPTER 14

¹One Sabbath day, Jesus went to eat dinner at the house of a prominent Pharisee. While He was there, Jesus was being carefully watched by everyone to see if He might break the Jewish Sabbath "traditions" again. ²At this dinner, Jesus encountered a man suffering from dropsy, which is an abnormal, painful swelling of his body. ³Jesus asked the Pharisees and experts in the Jewish religious law, "You have seen Me heal on the Sabbath before, and yet here you are, looking to see what I will do today. To test if you finally understand My message, let Me ask you a question: is it morally lawful and right in God's sight to heal on the Sabbath or not?"

⁴But the Jewish religious leaders remained silent and did not answer. When they refused to respond to Jesus, He reached out to touch the sick and disabled man and healed him, then sent him on his way to go about his life.

⁵Then Jesus turned and challenged those remaining, asking, "If you

had a child or a cow that fell into a well on the Sabbath, what would you do? Would you not rush to them and immediately try to pull them out? Why is it appropriate to do the 'work' of compassion in one situation and not another?" [6]They were at a loss for what to say, and, once again, they failed to respond to Jesus.

[7]As Jesus surveyed the U-shaped dinner table and observed how the guests had jockeyed to pick the seats of honor near the head of the table, He shared with them the following illustrative story to make a moral point: [8]"When someone invites you to a wedding feast, where should you sit? You should not take the highest seat of honor, for a person who is more distinguished than you may have been invited. [9]If so, the host who invited you both will come and say, 'You are in the wrong seat. Give this person your seat.' As we know, in our ancient Near-Eastern culture, one's identity and worth are directly connected to honor and shame. If the host has to ask you to move, you would have to find whatever seat is left at the end of the table, and then you would be humiliated!

[10]"Instead, when you are invited to a wedding feast, think more highly of others than yourself and take the lowest place at the foot of the table. Then, when the host comes, he will see you in too low of place, and he will say to you, 'Friend, we have a better seat for you that you should sit in.' Then you will not be shamed but honored in the presence of all the other guests. [11]And here is the point: those who exalt themselves will be humbled, and those who humble themselves will be exalted."

[12]After addressing the guests, Jesus turned to His host and said, "When you host a lunch or dinner, who should you be focused on serving? Do not invite your friends, brothers, extended family, and rich neighbors. If you do, they may invite you back to a party they host, and that will be your only reward. There is nothing morally commendable about serving those who can serve you back. [13]Instead, invite the poor, the disabled, the lame, and the blind. [14]Then you will be fortunate and viewed favorably in God's sight. Even though they cannot repay you, it is morally commendable to serve in this manner, and you will be repaid at the resurrection of all of the people who have been made righteous before God."

¹⁵When a man sitting at the table with Jesus heard these things, he said to Jesus, "Even though we have our differences, how great will it be when all of us who share a religious heritage and general belief in a Higher Power are feasting together as one with God in His fully established kingdom?"

¹⁶Jesus replied, "Do not be so quick to assume that everyone will be there in God's kingdom. Let Me share a story with you. There was a man who was preparing a great dinner party. He sent out many guest invitations, and many of them made reservations. ¹⁷However, when it was time for the dinner party, the man sent his servant out to give the invited guests a message, 'Come on in; the great banquet that I have prepared for you is now ready.'

¹⁸"However, the invited guests who had supposedly made reservations for the party began to make excuses and rudely backed out of coming to the great banquet. The first said, 'I just purchased a piece of property, and I must go out and inspect it. Even though I made a reservation with you before, this inspection is more important right now. Please excuse me from the dinner party.'

¹⁹"Another person said, 'I have just purchased five pairs of oxen. Even though I made a reservation with you before, I want to go and examine them now. Please excuse me from the dinner party.'

²⁰"Yet another guest said, 'I just got married. Even though I made a reservation with you before, I want to focus on enjoying my marriage now, so I cannot attend.'

²¹"The servant came back and reported these responses to his master. The master was furious that he had prepared such a great dinner party for these invited guests, yet they had all decided not to come. However, even though the original people were not going to feast, the master refused to waste the goodness of the grand banquet he had prepared. So, he told his servant, 'Go out quickly into the streets and alleys of the town and bring in the poor, the crippled, the blind, and the lame.'

²²"After the servant had returned, he said, 'Sir, I have done what you commanded. Many of those who know their need have responded to

the invitation. But you prepared such a large, grand banquet that there is still room for more people.'

²³"Then the master said to the servant, 'Go out to the roads and country lanes. Urge anyone you come across and find to come to my grand banquet. I want my entire house filled with people regardless of who they are or where they come from. ²⁴And let me assure you of this: not one of those people who were originally invited, made a reservation, and then backed out will get even the smallest taste of the great dinner I prepared for this party. They had their chance to respond, but it is too late for them now. They have missed out on the party I prepared for them.'"

### 5.6. The life of following Christ requires Jesus to be the main priority in one's life (14:25–35).

²⁵Large crowds were now traveling with Jesus. He turned around and said to them, ²⁶"If anyone comes to follow and learn from Me, then I must come first and be the main priority in your life. For example, if you had to choose between loving Me and hating everything else in comparison, you must choose to love Me. Even if it meant hating your father and mother, spouse, children, brothers and sisters, or even your own life, you must choose to love Me. Loyalty and commitment to following Me come first. Otherwise, you cannot be My disciple. ²⁷Anyone who does not carry their own cross and face rejection from the world and live as one dead to the world's values and lifestyles in order to follow Me cannot really be learning My ways and is not My disciple.

²⁸"Before beginning this path of following Me, you should consider the cost. For example, suppose someone wanted to begin a construction project. Should that person not first sit down and estimate the total cost of building it to make sure he has enough money? ²⁹Otherwise, when he has completed the foundation, he may realize he does not have enough money and is not able to finish it. All who see it will mock him, ³⁰saying, 'This person ridiculously began to build something he could not afford to finish.'

³¹"And consider another example. Suppose a nation was about to go

to war with another country. Should the nation's leaders not first sit down and consider whether their army of 10,000 could defeat another country's army of 20,000 soldiers that is double their size? ³²If the nation with the smaller military cannot see a path to victory, its leaders should send a delegation to discuss peace terms with the larger army while their enemy is still far away and before they attack. ³³Just like these two examples, if you cannot give up everything you have to follow Me, then you cannot learn from Me and be My disciple.

³⁴"Following Me also takes commitment and perseverance over time. Consider the function of salt. In our day, salt can maintain its usefulness for up to fifteen years. But what happens when salt loses its saltiness? Can it still function as salt or have those qualities restored? ³⁵No. Salt that has lost its saltiness is no good for the soil or even a pile of horse manure. Instead, the useless salt is just thrown away.

"You need to pay attention to what I am saying: anyone who has ears to hear should use them to listen and understand."

### 5.7. The life of following Christ calls one to have a compassionate heart and to seek out those who are lost (15:1–32).

#### 5.7.1. Following Christ calls one to seek out those who are lost (15:1–10).

## CHAPTER 15

¹By this time, tax collectors and other notorious "sinners" often came to listen to Jesus' teaching. ²But the Pharisees and teachers of the Jewish religious law were not happy about it. They thought Jesus associating with these people they perceived as "sinners" was a serious breach of what right living with God required. They complained, saying, "Why in the world does Jesus spent so much time associating with these obviously sinful people? He is even eating with them!"

³In reply, Jesus told this story:

⁴"Suppose a man had a hundred sheep, and he lost one of them. Would he not leave the ninety-nine other sheep out in the open country and go after the one lost sheep until he found it? ⁵When he finds the lost

sheep, he will joyfully pick it up, lay it on his shoulders, and carry it back to join the flock. He will rejoice the entire journey back. ⁶And when he arrives back at home, he will call all his friends and neighbors together and say, 'Let us have a party! Come and celebrate with me because I have found my lost sheep!' ⁷Here is a spiritual reality you can be assured of: there will be more rejoicing and celebration in the heavenly realm where God is over one sinner who turns from their sinful, selfish living and entrusts their life to God than over nighty-nine religiously devout people who have not drastically strayed too far from His way.

⁸"Or suppose a woman had ten coins, each worth at least one day's wages, but she lost one of them. Would she not grab a lamp and sweep the entire house diligently, searching for it until she found it? ⁹When she finds it, she will call all of her friends and neighbors together and say, 'Let us have a party! Come and rejoice with me because I have found my lost coin.' ¹⁰Here is a spiritual reality you can count on: there is incredible joy and celebration in the presence of God's angels over just one "notorious" sinner who turns from their sinful, selfish living and entrusts their life to following God and His way."

### 5.7.2. Following Christ calls one to have compassion for those who are lost (15:11–32).

¹¹Jesus was not done yet. He continued by telling another story to illustrate His point: "There was once a man who had two sons. ¹²The younger son said to his father, 'Father, I want my share of the inheritance from your estate now, before you die.' So, the Father divided his estate and wealth between the two sons.

¹³"A few days later, the younger son packed his bags and took off for a distant country with all he had. Once there, the younger son squandered all his money on wild and reckless living. ¹⁴After he had burned through all his money, a severe famine spread across the entire country. With no money left, he became desperate.

¹⁵"He went to a local farmer in this distant country and persuaded the farmer to hire him. The farmer gave him the only work he had

available, working in his fields to feed the pigs. The work was so disgusting that no one wanted to do it. This job was so filthy that it was viewed as causing moral uncleanness with God. $^{16}$The younger brother worked hard at this filthy job, but he was not earning enough to sustain himself. He did not even make enough to feed himself adequately. He was so hungry that he would have even eaten the leftover corncobs the pigs had eaten, but no one gave him any.

$^{17}$"As the younger brother reflected on his situation, he came to his senses. He said, 'Why am I living like this? Even my father's hired servants do not go hungry like this and have food to spare. Yet here I am, needlessly starving to death! $^{18}$I will go back home to my father. I will say to him, "Father, I have missed the mark with God in my life and have not lived the way He would have me to live. I have also missed the mark with you, not living my life in a way that would be pleasing to your eyes. $^{19}$Given what I have done, I am no longer worthy of being called your son, but I would greatly appreciate it if you could find enough grace to grant me a position as one of your hired servants."' $^{20}$With a firm change of mind and decision made, then the younger son got up and set out to return home.

"When he was still a long way off on the horizon, his father saw him. Rather than just sitting in his pride and waiting for the son to cross the field, the father was filled with compassion and love. He ran to his younger son, threw his arms around him, and embraced him with fatherly love.

$^{21}$"The son began to say to him, 'Father, I have missed the mark with both God and with you in my life and how I have lived. I am no longer worthy of being called your son.'

$^{22}$"But the father was so overjoyed that he interrupted his son and began shouting directions to his servants, 'Quickly! Bring out the best robe we have so that we can put cleaner and better clothes on my son. Put the family ring on his fingers and a nice pair of sandals on his feet. $^{23}$Also, get the fattest heifer we have, kill it, and cook it. We are going to have a big party to celebrate this joyous occasion. $^{24}$For my son has returned. I thought he was dead, but now here he is; he has come back home and is alive! He was lost, but now he is found.' And they began to celebrate.

²⁵"While all of this was happening and the younger son had been brought inside, the older son was outside working in the fields. As he returned home, he heard party music and saw dancing inside the house. ²⁶He called one of the servants over and asked him what was going on. ²⁷He said, 'Your younger brother has come back home. Your father has killed the best and fattest heifer we had in order to prepare a great feast to celebrate his safe return.'

²⁸"The older brother became enraged; he refused to go inside the house and join the celebration. Noticing that the older son was outside and refusing to come in, the father went out to try and talk some sense into him. But the older son would not listen. ²⁹The older son responded, 'This is preposterous and unbelievable! For many years I have been working hard for you and never once refused to do anything you wanted me to do. Yet, in all this time, you have never even killed your smallest animal to celebrate anything I have done for you with my friends. ³⁰But within hours of this son of yours coming home, the son who squandered all of his money—which was really your money—on prostitutes, what do you do? You kill the best and fattest heifer we have and prepare it in order to throw him a big party!'

³¹"The father said to his older son, 'Son, I am afraid you do not understand. You have been with me all these years, and all that I have has been yours. You have had access to everything I have and all the joys that come with it. ³²But your brother's situation has been different. It is only fitting for us to celebrate this tremendous occasion of his return and to be very happy because of it, for your brother was assumed to be dead but now is alive! He was lost, but now he is found!'"

### 5.8. The life of following Christ calls for one to be wise and generous with the resources God has given them (16:1–31).

*5.8.1. Following Christ calls for one to faithfully use the resources that God has given them (16:1–13).*

### CHAPTER 16

¹Jesus told His disciples another story to make a point: "There was a

wealthy man who had a financial manager handling his wealth. One day, a report came that the financial manager was wasting the wealthy man's money. ²So, the wealthy man called the financial manager in and asked him about it, saying, 'What is this I hear about you mishandling my money? Turn in the account books for my account, because I am not going have you be my financial planner any longer.'

³"Then the financial planner said to himself, 'Now that I have been fired and can no longer make a commission from these accounts, which was my only livelihood, what shall I do? I am not strong enough to work in construction or a manual labor job. I am too ashamed to beg from others. ⁴Ah, I know what I can do. Even though I have been removed from managing these accounts, I still have all my client contacts. They will likely welcome me into their houses.'

⁵"So he contacted each person who owed money to his previous employer. He asked the first, 'How much do you owe my boss?'

⁶"The debtor replied, 'I owe him nine hundred gallons of olive oil, which is worth about three years' wages.'

"The financial planner said to him, 'Take your bill. Let us quickly modify it and settle this account for half of what you owe, four hundred and fifty gallons.'

⁷"Then the financial planner said to another person who owed his previous employer money, 'How much do you owe my boss?'

"The debtor replied, 'I owe him a lot! One thousand bushels of wheat, which is about nine years' worth of wages.'

"The financial planner replied, 'Take your bill and let us settle the account for eighty percent of what you owe—approximately eight hundred bushels.'

⁸"When the wealthy man found out what was happening, what do you think he said about his former financial planner's dishonest actions? It may surprise you, but he actually admired the financial planner's shrewd and prudent steps to take care of himself. Many non-religious

people are indeed wiser and smarter in taking care of their physical, worldly, and financial wellbeing than religious people are in taking care of their inner, spiritual life and wellbeing.

⁹"Now here is the first lesson I want you to learn from this dishonest financial planner: use whatever resources God has given you to your spiritual benefit. If you have worldly wealth and use it in a generous way for others good, you will gain friends. And when a day comes when the money is gone (or the day when money does not matter any longer), you will be readily welcomed into God's eternal home, because this type of generous and godly personal character belongs there.

¹⁰"Here is a second lesson to learn from this story: one who is faithful with little things can be trusted with large things. Likewise, one who is dishonest with very little will be dishonest with a lot. ¹¹If you have not been faithful in handling worldly wealth, then who will trust you to handle the true wealth of spiritual things? ¹²If you have not been faithful to put someone else's resources to good use, then why should anyone think you will be generous and not selfish with your own resources?

¹³"Here is a third lesson to learn from this story: no one can serve two different masters that have diametrically opposed interests. Either you will hate one and love the other, or you will be devoted to one and despise the other. It is this simple: you cannot serve the interests of both God (who focuses on serving others) and money (which focuses on serving oneself)."

> 5.8.2. *Following Christ calls for one to recognize that He brings a new era of human living and trusts in Him as the source of what one values most in life (16:14–18).*

¹⁴The Pharisees, who were lovers of money, heard Jesus teach these things. They scoffed at what He said. ¹⁵Jesus said to them, "You like to appear holier than others. You like the outward appearance of looking like you are living right with God, but God knows your hearts. And God operates on a different value system, for what is highly valued by outward-facing and worldly-focused people is detestable in God's

sight.

¹⁶"The scriptural teachings in the Law and Prophets were your guide until John the Baptist arrived. However, since the arrival of John the Baptist, a new era of how God is working in the world has been proclaimed. This new era brings with it a new message, which is this: God's kingdom has come! His kingdom has been initiated, and the time for the fulfillment of God's promises has already begun. We no longer have to wait for God's deliverance. This message about God's kingdom is being communicated to all, and everyone is being given an insistent and urgent invitation to enter into it.

¹⁷"This new era and its message of a New Covenant between God and humankind do not contradict or destroy the Old Covenant teaching in the Law and Prophets. Instead, it shows that God is fulfilling the promises and hope found in the Old Covenant Scriptures. Every element of the Old Covenant Scriptures find their complete fulfillment in this new era of God's working and His message of a New Covenant between Himself and humankind. It would be easier for the sky above and the earth below to pass away than for the smallest point of God's Old Covenant Law not to be fulfilled in the new era of God's kingdom.

¹⁸"To see how the Old Covenant teaching and the new era of God's New Covenant have continuity, let us look at how the integrity called for in marriage in the New Covenant matches the Old Covenant. The new era teaches that anyone who makes a commitment in marriage, divorces his wife because he wants another woman, and then marries this other woman because he lusted after her commits adultery. A man who divorces his wife like this misses God's mark for their lives. Likewise, anyone who lusts after a divorced woman and marries her to fulfill his lust for her commits adultery. See how both the Old Covenant Scriptures and the New Covenant teachings on marriage match? They both state that everyone should take their marital commitments seriously and not just use the legalities of the divorce law to fulfill their lusts."

> 5.8.3. *Following Christ calls one to be generous in meeting human needs in this life because people's decisions about Him will have eternal consequences (16:19–31).*

¹⁹Jesus shared another story: "There once was a rich man who was dressed in the most expensive and highest fashion of the day who wallowed in luxurious consumption every day. ²⁰At this rich man's gate lay a poor man named Lazarus. He was covered with ulcerated sores. ²¹In his poor circumstances, he longed just to eat the scraps that fell from the rich man's table. He was in such a sad physical condition that even the dogs came and licked his sores (which also made him unclean in Jewish custom and unable to enter the place of worship).

²²"The time came when the poor man died, and he was carried by the angels to be by Abraham's side in the heavenly realm. The rich man also died, and he was buried. ²³In the realm of hell, where the rich man was in torment, he looked up and saw Abraham far away in the heavenly realm. He saw the poor man Lazarus by his side. ²⁴The rich man cried out, 'Father Abraham, please have pity on me! Send Lazarus to dip the end of his finger in water so that he can cool my tongue, for I am in utter agony in these flames.'

²⁵"But Abraham said, 'Son, remember that in your lifetime you had everything you wanted and Lazarus had nothing. In this great reversal, you have now discovered eternity's values: because of how he lived, now Lazarus is comforted here in the heavenly realm, and because of how you lived, you are now in the agony of hell. ²⁶Besides, there is a great and impenetrable chasm that has been fixed in place between these eternal realms. It has been established so that no one from the heavenly realm can cross over and come to you from there and so that no one from hell may cross over to us from where you are.'

²⁷"The rich man replied, 'Then I beg you, Father Abraham, if you cannot send Lazarus to me, please send Lazarus to my family. ²⁸I have five brothers. Please let Lazarus go and warn them so that they do not end up in this place of torment like me.'

²⁹"Father Abraham said, 'Those who are alive have the scriptural teachings of Moses and the Prophets. They have the same opportunity to respond to God's teaching while they live as you did. So let them listen to their teaching.'

[30]"The rich man replied, 'I know they have the scriptural teaching available to them, Father Abraham, but they are not listening to what God is saying through them. However, if someone from the dead goes back to tell them the truth about the eternal consequences of their choices, then they will turn from their sinful, selfish ways and trust their lives to God and follow His way.'

[31]"Father Abraham responded, 'If they do not listen to what God is saying through Moses and the Prophets, then they will not be convinced even if someone rises from the dead.'"

### 5.9. The life of following Christ will confront false teaching and require one to embody forgiveness, faith, and service (17:1–10).

## CHAPTER 17

[1]One day, Jesus said to His disciples, "There will always be snares and traps set to entice you to sin, which will cause you to miss God's mark for your life. But how divinely distressing and horrible it will be for the one who entices you into these traps and snares! [2]It would be better for that person to be thrown into the sea with a two-hundred-pound millstone tied around their neck than to cause people who, like little children, are helpless before God to fall into the trap of sin. For that person who is leading people astray, death would be better than facing God's judgment for their horrible actions. [3]So constantly pay attention and be alert to your teaching, and look out for each other!

"If another sins and misses God's mark in their life, express strong disapproval in an attempt to correct that person. If that person repents, turning from sin and turning back toward God, then forgive them as though they had never done anything wrong. [4]Even if a person's sins are directly and personally against you. Even if those sins against you are done seven times in a day. If they come back to you after each time they sin and ask for your forgiveness, you must forgive that person as though they had never committed even the first offense—as though they have never done anything wrong against you."

⁵Then the apostles—the twelve disciples appointed as Jesus' special ambassadors—said to the Lord, "Give us more faith or show us how to increase it."

⁶The Lord replied, "My primary concern is not the amount of faith you have, but whether you have authentic faith at all. If you have a genuine faith that is as small as a poppy or mustard seed, you could say to a mulberry or sycamore tree, 'Pull up your roots and be planted in the sea,' and it would obey you. So, I am not concerned about the quantity of your faith but the quality of it—that your faith is genuine and authentic.

⁷"My secondary concern is that your authentic faith would lead to humble service. For example, imagine one of you has a servant who comes in from plowing the fields and taking care of the sheep. After he has come in from doing his duty, would the master give him special treatment and say, 'You should come in and take a special place at the dinner table with me because you have been doing your job?' ⁸No. Instead, he would say, 'Since you have finished one of your tasks, now it is time for your next daily task. It is time to prepare for dinner. Please change your clothes and serve me while I drink and eat. Then, when your work is done, you can eat and drink.' ⁹In this situation, does the master give special thanks to the servant for doing what he was told to do? Of course not. ¹⁰It is to be the same way with you in your life with God. When you have done everything God wanted you to do, you should continue to have the attitude of a humble servant doing his work and say, 'We are merely unworthy servants possessing no special merit; we have simply been doing our duty.'"

### 5.10. The life of following Christ requires one to trust in God's plan and timing, and to be faithful in looking toward the King, His Kingdom, and the ultimate consummation of His rule (17:11–18:8).

*5.10.1. Following Christ calls for faith and gratitude, and the call to follow Him is freely available to everyone (17:11–19).*

¹¹As Jesus continued on His journey toward Jerusalem, He was passing along the border between Galilee and Samaria. ¹²As He entered into

one village, Jesus was approached by ten lepers. Even though they were supposed to remain isolated from other people because of their disease, they knew Jesus was approachable. However, they were also trying to honor the scripture in Leviticus 13:45-46 that commanded them not to mix with others. So, they called out to Jesus while from a distance. [13]The ten lepers called out in a loud, pleading voice, "Jesus, our Master, please have pity on us; show us Your mercy by healing us!"

[14]When Jesus saw them, He said, "When one has been healed, the Scriptures say in Leviticus 14:1-11 that you are to go and show yourself to the priest. So, do what they teach. Go and show yourselves to the priests." As they turned to go to the priests, they were all cleansed of their leprosy.

[15]When one of them saw that he was healed, he turned around and came back to Jesus. He praised God with a loud voice. [16]He laid himself prostrate on the ground at Jesus' feet and gave immense thanks for what Jesus had done for him. This man was a Samaritan, viewed by the Jewish people as a religiously despised half-breed because of his race (one they viewed as racially and religiously beyond God's grace and salvation).

[17]Then Jesus made a positive example of this Samaritan outcast's response to being healed by saying, "Did I not heal ten men? Where are the other nine? [18]Has no one returned to give thanks and praise to God except this cultural outcast and religiously despised foreigner?" [19]Then Jesus said to the man, "Please rise to your feet and go on your way. Your genuine and authentic faith—your trust and confidence in God—has healed you."

> 5.10.2. *Following Christ calls one to recognize and trust in the King and the hope of His kingdom that is present in His presence (17:20-18:8).*
>
> 5.10.2.a. Recognize that God's kingdom is in their midst (17:20-21).

[20]One day, with so much discussion about the kingdom of God occurring, the Pharisees were naturally curious. They asked Jesus a normal question that was debated continuously and always on their minds:

"When will the kingdom of God come?"

Jesus replied, "The coming of the kingdom of God—its initial inbreaking into this world—is not something that will come through apocalyptic means such as observable cosmic displays or undeniable visible signs. ²¹There will be no need to point to an unusual event and say, 'Look, here is a clear cosmic sign!" or 'There it is; there is the apocalyptic, undeniable thing that we have been looking for!' You can waste your time and energy looking for those undeniable, visible displays, but the reality is that the coming of God's kingdom and the hope it brings to the world has already begun. Right now, the inbreaking of God's kingdom is in your midst. In fact, it is standing right in front of you and within your reach."

> 5.10.2.b. Recognize that God's coming kingdom will be preceded by swift judgment (17:22-27).

²²Then Jesus said to His disciples, "It is natural to long for the undeniable, visible, and cosmic displays that signify the arrival of God's kingdom. You may long to see the kingdom come in such clear and powerful ways—and you can rest assured that one day it will arrive via apocalyptic means—but you do not need to worried about seeing it come in that way right now. If you are too preoccupied looking for apocalyptic signs, you will miss how God's kingdom is breaking into and active in the world right now. ²³Throughout your lives, you are going to hear people at various times say, 'Look at what just happened; there he is' or 'Here he is!' But do not pay any attention to these people trying to read the times for signs of the full, final, and ultimate arrival of God's kingdom. ²⁴You never have to worry about missing it. When that final time comes, it will be visible and evident to all. Everyone will know it and see it. Just as lightning flashes and lights up the sky from one edge of the horizon to the other and is seen by all, so it will be when the Son of Man comes one final time to fully and completely establish God's kingdom. ²⁵But before that time comes, there is something that has to happen in God's divine plan. First, the Son of Man must suffer many things and be rejected by the people of this generation.

²⁶"When the Son of Man arrives to bring the final judgment and to fully establish God's kingdom, in the days preceding the last ultimate

judgment on the earth, it will be like it was in the days of Noah. ²⁷Genesis 7 tells us in that time people were going about their everyday lives; they were eating, drinking, and marrying and gave little attention or thought to God. They carried on, just enjoying life however they saw fit until the day when, as directed by God, Noah entered the ark. Then the flood suddenly came and destroyed them all.

²⁸"The world's mindset will be similar to how it was in days of Lot in Sodom and Gomorrah mentioned in Genesis 19. People were going about their daily living; they were eating, drinking, buying and selling things, farming and building, and were paying no attention to God. ²⁹They continued in this pattern of living until the day when Lot, as directed by God, left the city of Sodom. Then raging, consuming fire and burning sulfur suddenly rained down from the skies above and destroyed them all.

³⁰"When the Son of Man comes to bring God's final judgment and to fully establish God's kingdom, it will be just like these two examples. It will be sudden, decisive, final, and complete. ³¹To get an idea of how swiftly this will happen, on that day, a person who is on the deck of his or her house will not have time to go down into their house and pack. A person who is out in the field working will not have time to go back home for anything. ³²Remember how Lot's wife tried to look back when the time of God's judgment came in Genesis 19, and she was destroyed? Similarly, when the Son of Man comes and brings God's final judgment, there will not be any time left to make any kind of arrangements; there will be no time to change anything. With this urgency in mind, you should not be tied to the things of this world that will keep you from being prepared for God's judgment when it comes. ³³For whoever seeks to hold on to the life they have on this earth and values it more than living for God will lose an ultimate life with God in His kingdom. But whoever values living for God and considers it to be more valuable than anything else in this world will gain an ultimate life with God in His kingdom.

³⁴"I cannot underscore this point enough: how that Day—the Day when the Son of Man arrives to bring God's final judgment and establishes His full kingdom—will be a decisive day. There will be two people sitting on a couch; one will be taken, and the other will be left

behind. ³⁵There will be two people working in the same area to prepare a meal; one will be taken, and the other will be left behind." ³⁶[Some manuscripts include: "There will be two men working in the same field; one will be taken, and the other will be left behind."]

³⁷Then the disciples asked Jesus, "Where will definitive judgment take place?"

Jesus replied, "Instead of wondering where it will happen, you should be focused on the devastating and eternal consequences of those who are ready for when that day comes. Just as a dead body causes vultures to gather around it, so the people left behind from the judgment will be sitting there, ready to be devoured."

> 5.10.1.c. Recognize that God's kingdom calls people to persistent and enduring faith (18:1-8).

## CHAPTER 18

¹One day, Jesus told His disciples a parable (a story with a moral point) to help them understand how they should always pray and never lose heart in the persistence of their faith. ²He said, "There was a judge in a certain town who neither cared about honoring God nor showing Him respect; he also did not care what others thought about him. ³In this town, there was a widow who approached this judge repeatedly with the same plea: 'I have an adversary who is taking advantage of me. Please give me justice and settle this dispute.'

⁴"For some time, the judge had ignored her plea and refused to do anything about it. But finally he gave in, saying to himself, 'Even though I do not care about honoring God or showing Him respect, and I could care less what people think of me, ⁵yet because this woman continually pesters me, I will see that she gets the justice she seeks. Otherwise, I might end up black-and-blue from the constant pounding of her requests.'"

⁶Then the Lord said, "You can learn an important lesson from this unjust judge. When the unjust judge, who did not care about anyone else, received a constant plea, he granted the request. ⁷If an unjust and

uncaring judge can grant justice, how much more do you think God, who is full of love and compassion, will give justice to people who belong to Him, to those who plea and cry out to Him day and night? Do you think a loving God will just blow off your request and not respond? ⁸I tell you this truth you can count on: God will give justice to His people quickly! But I wonder, when the Son of Man comes to establish ultimate justice, will He find this kind of steady and persistent faith on the earth?"

### 5.11. The life of following Christ requires faithful humility and trusting in the Father for all things in life (18:9–30).

#### 5.11.1. Following Christ calls one to live a faithful life of humility before God (18:9–17).

⁹Then Jesus told another parable that highlighted what a true response to trusting in God looks like. He told this parable to some who never lacked for an overabundance of self-righteousness and who had persuaded themselves they were better than everyone else:

¹⁰"Two men went into the Temple to pray. One was a Pharisee (a publicly respected, Jewish, religious leader) and the other was a despised tax collector (a person viewed as an immoral and societal low-life).¹¹The Pharisee stood up proudly and prayed: 'I thank You, God, that I am not like other people. I am not greedy or trying to rob people of money; I am not unjust; I do not commit adultery; and thank goodness I am not like this tax collector. ¹²How great it is that I fast voluntarily twice a week and that I tithe, giving a tenth of all my income to God.'

¹³"Meanwhile, the tax collector stood at a distance. He assumed he had no merit that made him worthy to approach God. When he prayed, he would not even look up toward heaven (which was a custom in Jewish prayers). Instead, the tax collector beat his chest as a sign of contrition and said, 'God, I do not deserve Your kindness, but please have mercy on me; please pull the covers over all the ways in which I missed Your mark for my life, for I am a sinner.'

¹⁴"Which one of these do you think was right with God? I tell you this reality: this humble tax collector—the perceived notorious

sinner—not the self-righteous Pharisee went home justified with God. Meaning, God looked at him as though he had never done anything wrong. Remember this reality: everyone who exalts themselves will be humbled, and those who humble themselves will be exalted."

> 5.11.2. *Following Christ calls for one to follow the example of a child, to have a simple, trusting, and humble faith in the Heavenly Father (18:15-17).*

[15] One day, people brought little children to Jesus because they thought that He might touch them and impart some kind of special favor upon them. When the disciples saw the children, they rebuked these people for wanting to waste Jesus' time on unimportant little children. [16] But Jesus intervened, calling out to them and saying, "Let the little children come to me. Do not hinder them, for the kingdom of God belongs to people who are like these children. [17] I tell you this truth, anyone who does not receive My rule in their life and My kingdom with simple trust, humility, and dependency like a child will never enter it."

> 5.11.3. *Following Christ calls for one to trust in the Father above all other things in one's life (18:18-30).*

[18] One day, a government official asked Jesus, "Good Teacher, You are morally upright and knowledgeable about God; I have a question for You about my standing with God. What must I do to inherit eternal life and be a part of God's kingdom forever?"

[19] Jesus replied, "Why are you calling Me good? I am not one who will respond to flattery, and besides, no one is good and morally perfect except God alone. [20] But to answer your question, you know what God's commandments found in Exodus 20:12-16 and Deuteronomy 5:16-20 say: 'You shall not commit adultery; you shall not murder; you shall not steal; you shall not speak false things; honor your father and mother.'"

[21] The man replied, "Indeed, I have kept all of these Old Testament commands since I was a youth until now."

²²When Jesus heard his response, He said, "Then there is only one thing left for you to do. Sell everything that you have and give all the money to the poor. This action will demonstrate that your trust, confidence, and allegiance is completely in God and not in your wealth and possessions. Then, after you have sold everything and given it to the poor, come and follow Me, learning from Me how to walk with God."

²³When the man heard Jesus' challenge, he became sad and sorrowful, because he was very rich and was not about to let go of what he had. ²⁴When Jesus saw the man's reaction, He said, "How hard and difficult it is for those who have wealth to come under God's rule and enter His kingdom! ²⁵It is easier for a large camel to go through the tiny eye of a needle than for a rich person to come under God's rule and enter His kingdom."

²⁶Those who heard this teaching were flabbergasted. They said, "We have always thought being rich was a sign of God's special favor on a person. If a rich person cannot get into God's kingdom, then who in the world can be saved?"

²⁷Jesus replied, "While it is impossible for human beings to produce in themselves the type of heart change required by God, it is not impossible for God to produce the kind of heart change necessary to enter His kingdom."

²⁸Then Peter said to Jesus, "We, your disciples, have left our homes and everything to follow You. Have we done all that's required to enter God's kingdom?"

²⁹Jesus replied, "Let Me tell you this certain reality: there is no one who has entrusted their entire life and welfare to Me who will fail to enter into the kingdom family and receive the gift of eternal life with God. No one who has left home, spouse, brothers and sisters, parents, or children for the sake of the kingdom of God ³⁰will fail to receive many times more than what they sacrificed, both in their present experience and in the eternal life with God in the age that is to come."

## 5.12. The life of following Christ requires faith and calls for one to trust in God's plan (18:31–19:44).

> *5.12.1  Following Christ calls one to look for and see what God is doing even if one's expectations are different or if one is slow to see His work; a blind man can see what no one else does (18:31–43)*

³¹Then Jesus took aside the twelve specially chosen disciples entrusted to be His authoritative messengers. He said to them, "Pay careful attention to what I am about to say. We are on the last section of our journey toward Jerusalem. When we are in Jerusalem, many things are going to happen. But know that they are all part of God's divine plan. Everything written by the Prophets in the Scriptures about what will happen to the Son of Man will be fulfilled. ³²He will be handed over to the Roman Gentiles. Shamefully, they will mock Him, insult Him, and spit on Him. ³³After they have severely beaten Him with a flogging, they will kill Him. But on the third day, He will rise from the dead to live again."

³⁴But the apostles did not understand what Jesus meant. His words did not fit with their expectation of the Son of Man being a political warrior-king who would conquer the world and its powers. At this time, they did not comprehend God's larger plan and how suffering, death, and rising from the dead could be part of it. They did not understand how God would inaugurate His kingdom and complete the Jewish faith through these events.

³⁵As Jesus approached Jericho, a blind man was sitting by the road and begging. ³⁶When he heard the noise of a crowd going past, the blind man asked what was happening. ³⁷They told him, "Jesus of Nazareth is passing by."

³⁸Then the blind man began crying out loud to Him, saying, "Jesus, You are the Son of David who has the power and authority to heal all things. Please take pity on my condition and have mercy on me!"

³⁹The people traveling in the front of Jesus' entourage rebuked this blind man. They thought he was of too low social standing to be worth

Jesus' time and told him to be quiet. Yet the blind man only shouted louder, "Son of David, You have the power and authority to heal all things. Please have mercy on me!"

⁴⁰When Jesus heard the man, He stopped and ordered the blind man be brought to Him. When the blind man was near, Jesus asked, ⁴¹"What is it that you want Me to do for you?"

The man replied, "Lord, please let me receive my sight back; I want to see again!"

⁴²Jesus said to the blind man, "At this very moment, you will receive your sight back. Your faith has healed you!" ⁴³Immediately, the formerly blind man could see again. From that moment on, he followed Jesus in order to learn from Him and to give God praise for the great thing He had done. When all the people saw the blind man's healing, they also gave praise to God.

> 5.12.2. Following Christ calls one to recognize that He has come to seek and offer salvation to everyone (19:1–10).

## CHAPTER 19

¹Later on, Jesus entered Jericho and was passing through the town on His way to Jerusalem. ²In Jericho, there was a man named Zacchaeus. He was the lead supervisor—the chief—of all the tax collectors in the region. He took a commission from all the taxes that were collected. As a result, Zacchaeus was very rich. However, many people in the region considered his wealth to be corruptly gained. ³Zacchaeus was eager to see Jesus, but he was short and could not see over the crowd. ⁴When he realized he was not going to be able to see over the crowd, Zacchaeus decided to run ahead of Jesus' traveling entourage and climbed up into a sycamore tree so that he would be able to see Jesus when He passed by.

⁵When Jesus arrived at that spot, He looked up and said, "Zacchaeus, hurry up and come down here. I am destined to stay at your house today." ⁶Zacchaeus was incredibly excited to be noticed and to receive this news and honor. He quickly came down from the tree. Zacchaeus

then took Jesus to his house and was delighted to have Him there as his guest.

⁷When the people who were watching Jesus saw what He was doing, they were indignant. They grumbled, "Why in the world has Jesus associated Himself with this person who is well-known for wrongdoing and notorious for living and doing sinful things that would not please God?"

⁸While these observers were grumbling, Zacchaeus stood up and declared with a solemn and sincere voice, "In appreciation for You associating with me, and because I have a new relationship with You, Lord, I want to go above and beyond in giving away my wealth. I will give half of my wealth to the poor. Also, if I have cheated anyone out of anything, I will pay them back four times what I took."

⁹Jesus responded, "Today, we have seen this man's heart and mind changed in his relationship to God. The result: salvation has come to this home, for Zacchaeus is no longer a social outcast or one to be looked down upon as an immoral person or notorious sinner. Instead, Zacchaeus has shown that he is a true son of Abraham, one who has faith in God and who belongs to the generations of God's family. ¹⁰The Son of Man—the One who brings God's salvation to His people—does not show favoritism toward anyone; instead, He has come to seek and save those who know they are lost."

> 5.12.3. *Following Christ calls one to a life of faithful service and stewardship under His rule and within His kingdom (19:11–27).*

¹¹While the crowd was listening to Jesus, He wanted to drive home a spiritual reality for them. Jesus was approaching both Jerusalem and the end of His journey. Before arriving there, He wanted to address people's preconceived notions about the Christ, the Messiah, the One from God who would bring salvation to His people. They had the preconceived notion that the Christ would be a political warrior-king who would overthrow all the rulers of the world through His military might. So, Jesus told them this story to try and correct their misconception and help them understand His authority, expectation, and how

His judgment would work. ¹²Jesus said, "There was a descendant of a royal family who was living in a distant land far away from the main ruler and capital city. The descendant had not yet been appointed as king of his land. So he traveled to the emperor and capital city to be appointed king. ¹³But before leaving, the soon-to-be king called together ten of his business managers. He gave each one of them ten minas, which was roughly equivalent to one-third of an annual salary. The soon-to-be king instructed them, 'Use this money to engage in profitable business until I return.'

¹⁴"Even though this man was the soon-to-be king over their land, the citizens hated him. They sent a delegation to the capital city to oppose his rule, saying, 'We do not want this man to be our king and rule over us.' ¹⁵However, he was their chosen and appointed king, and he returned home to his people. When he arrived back among his people, he called in the servants to whom he had given money to invest; he wanted to find out how their investments and actions in their business dealings had paid off.

¹⁶"The first manager came before him and reported, 'Sir, I took the ten minas you gave me and earned a 100 percent return on the investment.'

¹⁷"The king responded, "Well done! You have done great work! Since you have been trustworthy in this small managerial task, I can trust you with more. I will trust you to be the governor over ten cities.'

¹⁸"The second manager came before the king and said, 'Sir, I took the ten minas you gave me and earned a fifty percent return on investment.'

¹⁹"The king replied, 'Well done! I will trust you to be the governor over five cities.'

²⁰"Then another manager came before the king and said, 'Sir, here is all your money back. I kept it hidden in a safe place. ²¹I was afraid to invest your money, because I know you are a hard leader with high standards, even taking out what you did not put in and reaping what you did not sow.'

²²"The king replied, 'Your own words condemn you. If you know my

character and that I have high expectations, one who takes out what I did not put in and reaps what I did not sow, ²³then why did you not at least deposit my money in the bank? At least then the money would have gained some interest. You claim to know my character and to have a relationship with me, but the reality is you do not know me at all. If you really knew me and wanted to honor me, your actions would have been different. You may have some kind of loose association and knowledge of me, but that is not enough. If you know me and my character, it will move you to action.'

²⁴"Then the king turned to the other managers standing nearby and said, 'Take the money away from this one who does not really know me. Give his money to the one who previously had ten minas and produced a 100 percent return on investment.'

²⁵"Upon hearing this, those listening responded, 'But Lord, why give that manager more? He already has 100 percent more than the original ten minas!'

²⁶"'Yes, that is right,' the king replied. 'Everyone who manages well what they have been given will be given more. However, for the one who does not manage well what they have been given, even what they have will be taken away from them.'

²⁷"Then the king turned his attention to his enemies who had protested and fought against his rule. He said, 'For all these enemies of mine who did not want me to rule over them, bring them here and slaughter them right in front of me.'"

> 5.12.4. *Following Christ calls one to follow a humble King who fulfills God's plan and rules a different kind of kingdom (19:28–44).*

²⁸After Jesus had finished telling that story, He traveled onward, heading toward Jerusalem. ²⁹As He approached the towns of Bethpage and Bethany, on the hill called the Mount of Olives (which is two miles east of Jerusalem), He sent two of his disciples out with these instructions, ³⁰"Go into the village in front of you. As you enter it, you will see a young donkey tied there that no one has ever ridden. Untie that

donkey and bring it back here to Me. ³¹If anyone asks you, 'What do you think you are doing with that donkey?' reply, letting them know it is not an unusual request, by saying, 'The Lord needs it.'"

³²Then the two disciples went on ahead of the entourage and found the donkey just as Jesus had told them they would. ³³As they were untying the donkey, its owners asked them, "What do you think you are doing with that donkey?"

³⁴The two disciples replied, "The Lord needs it."

³⁵After acquiring it, the two disciples brought the donkey back to Jesus. They threw their outer cloaks on the donkey's back and helped Jesus mount it. ³⁶As Jesus rode along, making a humble, non-militant, peaceful, and servant-like arrival, the people honored Him and His arrival by spreading their cloaks on the road to give Him a royal welcome.

³⁷When Jesus reached the point where the road starts to go down the hill from the Mount of Olives, the whole entourage of Jesus' followers began to joyfully and loudly praise God for all the mighty things they had seen. ³⁸To celebrate the arrival of the One who brings God's authority, they sang out the hope of Psalm 118:26:

"Worthy of all honor and favor is the King who comes, the One who is appointed by God and who is full of His character! In the heavenly realm where God is, there is peace and freedom from all distress. Its value and worth are so great that we cannot even begin to comprehend its greatness!"

³⁹Some Pharisees were among the crowd and were offended by these regal, God-like claims toward Jesus. They said to Him, "Teacher, are You going to let Your followers say such absurd things, claiming that you are the Messiah who will save them? You must rebuke them!"

⁴⁰Jesus replied to them, "Do not be so hard-headed. You should realize that even if they stopped their praise and became silent, the stones of this road would shout out My praise."

⁴¹As He approached the city and Jerusalem came into view, Jesus wept over the many people there. ⁴²With tears, Jesus said, "Oh, how I wish all of you had paid attention and realized that the 'Day' you have longed for—the day when God brings His peace to all the world—is now here. But now it is too late to respond; you had your chance. You did not use your eyes to see what was right in front of you, and now you have missed it. ⁴³By refusing to see Him and respond to Him in faith, you have made a frightful choice with tragic consequences. A time is coming upon you, Jerusalem—a city that symbolizes all people of Old Covenant Israel—when your enemies will set up an artillery barricade around you and lay a siege upon you on every side. ⁴⁴They will tear you down, smashing your city, and even the children within it, to the ground. They will not leave one stone intact because you did not recognize the time when God personally visited you. You failed to respond to His offer of salvation."

**6. Discovering the Savior's victory: Jesus fulfills God's plan to make salvation available to all through His innocent suffering and by His vindication through His resurrection [In Jerusalem] (19:45–24:53).**

    **6.1. Hold onto the truth: Even though Jesus is challenged, questioned, and surrounded in controversy by human beings who do not understand Him, God is fulfilling His plan to bring salvation to the world (19:45–21:4).**

        *6.1.1. Jesus is challenged about the source of His authority (19:45–20:8).*

⁴⁵When Jesus entered Jerusalem, He went straight to the Temple, which was the central location of Old Covenant Jewish religious worship and life. To the Jewish people, the Temple represented God's physical presence among; it was also the place where people would make animal sacrifices, shedding an animal's blood to cover over their sins so that God might see them as innocent. As people came to the Temple area to make these atoning sacrifices, they often bought sacrificial animals in the Temple court. They purchased these animals with Roman currency that had been exchanged to Hebrew shekels, which was a Jewish currency, the only one they considered pure enough to be allowed

in the Temple. As people exchanged their currency, some expected surcharges existed, like the ones that cover the Temple priest's services. However, many times, the currency exchangers took advantage of those needing to exchange money and charged them exorbitant amounts.

When Jesus entered the Temple, He saw this practice and began to drive out all those who were selling animals for sacrifices. $^{46}$He said, "God has declared in Isaiah 56:7 that 'My Temple is intended to be a place dedicated to prayer.' But as Jeremiah 7:11 declares, 'You have turned it into a place where you rob people of money.'"

$^{47}$After this encounter, Jesus continued to teach in the Temple daily. However, the leading priests, the teachers and legal experts of the Jewish religious law, and the Jewish civic leaders began looking for a way to legally kill Jesus. $^{48}$Yet they could not find a way to do it because all the people were interested in Jesus's teaching and intrigued by everything He said.

## CHAPTER 20

$^{1}$One day, as Jesus was teaching the people in the Temple and communicating the good news of God's kingdom that was now at hand, the leading priests, teachers and scholars of the religious law, and civic elders came up to Him. $^{2}$They demanded, "You are making huge, divine statements that call the essentials of our religious life and worship into question. What credentials do You have? What credentials have You earned that allow you to make such statements? Who has given You the authority to say all of these things?"

$^{3}$Jesus replied, "If you think your credentials and authority are so great, let Me first ask you a question. $^{4}$Tell Me, was John the Baptist's baptism authorized by heaven, or was it purely of human origin?"

$^{5}$They discussed the matter among themselves and weighed the public perception of their response. They thought, "If we say, 'It was authorized by heaven,' then He will ask, 'If a prophet like John can receive direct authority from heaven, then why do you not believe John's teaching?' $^{6}$However, if we say, 'It is purely of human origin,' then all of the people will stone us to death because they are convinced John was a prophet from God. Neither one of these answers will play well publicly, and both will make us look bad."

⁷So, they finally answered, saying, "We do not know where John the Baptist's authority came from."

⁸Jesus responded to them, saying, "Since you cannot determine if one's authority is from heaven or from human origins, then I see no reason to answer your question and tell you where My authority to do these things comes from."

> 6.1.2. Jesus challenges people's perspective on how they view the history of God's work and activity in the world (20:9-19).

⁹Then Jesus turned to the people and began to tell them this story with a moral point: "There was a man who planted a vineyard. He rented it out to some tenant farmers and then left. He went away to another country for a long time. ¹⁰When harvest time came, he sent a servant back to collect his share of the crop. But the tenant farmers beat the servant and sent him away empty-handed. ¹¹Then the owner sent another servant back to collect his share of the crop, but they treated him shamefully, beat him up, and sent him away empty-handed. ¹²So, he sent a third servant, but they severely wounded him and threw him out on the street.

¹³"The owner of the vineyard was perplexed by the situation. He wondered: 'What do I have to do to get through to these people? I know! I will send my one and only son. Surely they will respect him.'

¹⁴"But when the tenant farmers saw that the owner had sent his son, in their twisted logic, they thought they had an opportunity to gain the property for themselves. They said, 'This son is the heir. Let us kill him because then we will be next in line to receive this land.' ¹⁵So, they dragged the owner's son out of the vineyard and killed him.

"Now, what do you think the owner of the vineyard will do when he finds out what they did to his son? ¹⁶He will come and utterly destroy those tenants, and, after killing those wicked tenants, he will give the vineyard over to an entirely different group of other people."

When the people in the crowd heard this story, they understood that Jesus was talking about them—that the vineyard was God's promise and the, the people of Israel, were the tenants. So they responded, "What a horrible outcome; God would never do that to us! Surely this would never happen among us; we would never do such terrible things!"

[17]Jesus looked directly at them and said, "If you think something like this could never happen to you, then what does this part of Psalm 118 mean, which says:

> The stone that the builders rejected has become the chief cornerstone that determines the entire foundation.

[18]"Anyone who does not build on the foundation on God's chosen cornerstone will stumble over it. Their lives will be shattered into pieces. And the weight of the stone will be so heavy that when it falls upon them, it will utterly crush them."

[19]The teachers of the Old Covenant Jewish religious law and the leading priests immediately wanted to arrest Jesus; they knew He had spoken this parable directly at them. However, with the crowd so enthralled by what Jesus was saying, they feared how the crowd might react if they arrested Him. So, they waited.

> 6.1.3. *Jesus is challenged by a plot against Him and remains innocent when overcoming a politically incriminating trap (20:20-26).*

[20]After this encounter, these religious leaders continued to keep a close watch on Jesus. They sent spies into the crowds who pretended to be sincere, but they were only there to catch Jesus saying something that could be used against Him. They hoped Jesus would say something subversive against Roman rule so they could report it to the Roman governor and let him use his power and authority to put an end to Jesus. [21]These spies, faking good intentions, asked Jesus a question: "Teacher, we know that You speak and teach what is right, that You are

not influenced by anyone's title or position. You just teach God's truth as it is. ²²So, is it lawful and right for us to pay taxes to Caesar or not?"

²³Jesus saw right through their deceptive question and ill-intent. He said to them, ²⁴"Somebody pull out a Roman denarius, a common coin that we all likely have, and show it to Me. Whose image and inscription are on it?"

They replied, "Caesar's."

²⁵Jesus replied, "Then give back to Caesar what is Caesar's, and give back to God what belongs to God."

²⁶They were amazed at such an insightful answer and decided to keep quiet after that. They realized they were not going to be able to trap Jesus into saying something politically incriminating in front of the people.

> 6.1.4. Jesus addresses questions on the afterlife and resurrection (20:27-40).

²⁷Then some of the Sadducees, those who were scholars of the Jewish Old Covenant Law, came to Jesus. The Sadducees were known for having an overly-rationalistic belief system because they only recognized the Torah, the first five books of the Old Covenant, as Scripture. They also denied and rejected that there will be a resurrection of the body. ²⁸To highlight their lack of belief in a resurrection, they asked Jesus a question based on a ludicrous story: "Teacher, Moses gave us instruction in Genesis 38:8 and Deuteronomy 25:5 that if a man's brother dies, leaving a wife with no children, then he should marry the widow and have a child with her to carry on his brother's name. ²⁹Well, let us suppose there are seven brothers. The first brother married a woman, but he died and left her childless. ³⁰The next oldest brother married the widow to fulfill his duty, but he also died and left her childless. ³¹Then a third brother did the same and died, leaving her childless. This pattern continued with all seven brothers until they had all died and left the woman without a child. ³²Eventually, the wife died as well. ³³So here is the question: at the resurrection, since she was married to all seven brothers, whose wife will she actually be?"

³⁴Jesus replied, "There are two issues to discuss in your question: the nature of the afterlife and whether there will be a resurrection. First, let us address the nature of the afterlife using marriage as an example. In the present age, marriage exists; people marry and are given in marriage. ³⁵However, for those who are considered worthy to be included in the age to come—those who will experience life with God after the resurrection from the dead—marriage will no longer be a concern for them. ³⁶In the age to come, people will not die. They will have a new eternal existence in the heavenly realm like the angels. They will experience a complete and satisfying new life in a new resurrected body; they will exist in a perfect relationship with God as one of His children. That is the nature of the afterlife with God.

³⁷"Now, let us examine the other aspect of this question: will there be a resurrection or not? From the Torah, in Exodus 3:2-6, the passage about the burning bush, even Moses proved there is a resurrection from the dead. In that passage, God said to Moses that the Lord is the God of Abraham, Isaac, and Jacob. As God spoke to Moses in that Scripture, He was saying that He is still actively the God of those deceased patriarchs of the faith. By talking about them in the active, present tense, God was implying they must still be alive or present somehow in His midst, something that is only possible if there is, in fact, a physical, bodily resurrection from the dead. ³⁸After all, He is not the God of the dead but of the living. Through Him and with Him, they are all alive in a physically resurrected body."

³⁹Some of the Sadducees recognized Jesus' solid insight and responded, "That is a really good answer!" ⁴⁰They did not dare to ask Jesus any more of their questions designed to make Him stumble.

> 6.1.5. Jesus challenges His accusers with a theological question about the identity of the Messiah that they cannot answer (20:41-44).

⁴¹Then Jesus decided to ask them a question, saying, "How is that people can say the Christ—the anointed Messiah who will decisively save God's people—is also the son of David? ⁴²In Psalms 118:1, David writes:

The Mighty Lord said to the Lord [David],
"sit at My right hand in close relationship with Me. And you will be someone with great authority because of your special relationship and proximity to Me.
⁴³Sit in this position—at My right hand, the place of power—until I defeat your enemies and make them a footstool for your feet."

⁴⁴"If David addresses the Mighty Lord—the Messiah—as someone who is much more powerful and authoritative than he is, how can the Mighty Lord (or Messiah) also be his son, one of his descendants? In our culture, a father does not bow to his son, so how can one of David's descendants be the Mighty Lord who is His superior?"

> 6.1.6. *Jesus provides a final warning about the need to respond to His truth by contrasting one wrong way (led by personal pride in accomplishment) and one right way (led by personal humility in generous giving) (20:45–21:4).*

⁴⁵Then, with all the people still listening, Jesus wanted to contrast two different ways of responding to Him. Jesus warned His disciples: ⁴⁶"Beware of the teachers of the religious law. They are prideful! They like to walk around in special robes that set them apart from everyone else; they love for other people to greet them with flattering words in the marketplace because of their status and position. They love to sit in the best, most honored seats, whether at the religious place of worship or during banquets. ⁴⁷But the entire time, as they pursue these positions, they are nothing more than hypocrites. They cheat widows out of their property and pretend to be holier-than-thou by making long, passionate public prayers. But do not worry: God knows their hypocrisy. In the end, they will be severely punished for it.

## CHAPTER 21

¹While Jesus was in the Temple, He saw rich people putting their gifts to support the Temple operations into the offering receptacles in the Temple courtyard. ²As He watched, Jesus saw a poor widow approach the offering receptacles. She put in two very small copper coins worth about one half-hour of minimum wage labor. ³Jesus said

to those near Him, "I tell you this truth: this poor widow has given a larger offering than anyone else today, and I am not just talking about the amount. ⁴While everyone else gave out their abundance or surplus, this woman—even though she needed the money to live on and no one noticed her action—humbly gave out of her poverty, giving everything she had. Do you see the differences in their responses toward God?"

> **6.2. Be informed and encouraged: The old ways are broken and will come to a devastating end, but God is bringing a new way to be right with Him, which will be available to all people; keep one's eyes open, God's victory is coming through Christ (21:5-38).**

> *6.2.1. The old way is broken; a devastating end will come to it (21:5-19).*

⁵Later, some of Jesus' disciples began talking about how amazing the structure of the Temple was, with tremendous stone masonry and beautiful memorial artwork and many other gifts and offerings dedicated to God. But Jesus said to them, ⁶"Do not be so enamored by what you see here. The days are coming when that building will be demolished; every stone in it will be toppled over creating a huge pile of rubble."

⁷They responded, "Teacher, when will these things happen? Will there be a sign that lets us know when they are about to take place?"

⁸Jesus replied, "Be on guard and watch out for false doomsday predictors who will lead you astray. Many will come claiming to be the appointed One who has special insight and revelations from God. They will say, 'I am the Messiah who has all the answers' and 'The end times have come.' But do not fall for what they say; do not follow their teaching. ⁹When you hear of wars and various uprisings, there could be the temptation to think the sky is falling. But do not be frightened. These types of things are going to happen throughout human history; there is no reason to panic about the end times when they do. Simply put: these things happening are not immediate signs of the end times,

just reminders to be ready."

¹⁰Then Jesus continued: "For example, nation will rise against nation; kingdoms will fight against kingdoms. ¹¹There will be earthquakes, famines, and deadly epidemics and pandemic diseases throughout the world. There will be many terrifying events throughout history and devastating storms from the skies. But all of these things are just general reminders to be ready, to always be prepared for the end of life. They are not special or supernatural 'signs from heaven' about when the end times will occur.

¹²"Before the ends times comes, there are some general things you should expect to happen that should kickstart your preparation for the end times and remind you always to be prepared for it. The first thing you can expect is persecution. The Jewish religious leaders will seize you, drag you out of the synagogues, and throw you into prison. You will be brought to stand trial before Roman kings and governors for capital offenses—all because you are one of My followers. ¹³When this persecution occurs, it will the time for you to tell them about all you have seen, heard, know, and witnessed. ¹⁴But please put your mind at ease; do not worry now about how to answer the charges they will bring against you. ¹⁵For I will give you the words of wisdom you need so that none of your adversaries will be able to contradict or refute you. ¹⁶You should expect to encounter persecution from people who are close to you—parents, brothers and sisters, relatives, and friends. Some of you will even be killed by these 'loved ones.' ¹⁷Unfortunately, many people will hate you because you follow Me. ¹⁸But guess what? God protects you now, and He will protect you then. Even if death should come to you, you are in God's eternal care; no one can ultimately harm you. God's ultimate and eternal protection is so complete that you can rest assured not even a single hair on your body is outside of His care. ¹⁹So, stand firm in your faith; remain steadfast in your patient endurance through everything you endure. By doing so, you demonstrate your faith and will win the fulfilled life, the kind of life that will last throughout eternity, the kind of life your soul longs for.

> 6.2.2. *The old center of religious life will shift from a building to a person (21:20:24).*

[20]"The of persecution of My followers is the first thing that should kickstart your preparation for the end times, but that will just be the beginning. After the persecution of My followers begins, you will see some devastating things happen here in Jerusalem that should also remind you to always be ready for the end. When you see an army surrounding Jerusalem and laying siege to the city, you will know the time of its destruction—and the fall of Jerusalem—has come. [21]During this time, those living in Judea should flee and hide in the mountains. Those living in Jerusalem should get out as quickly as they can. Those living in the country should not enter Jerusalem and avoid it at all costs. [22]When you see this siege of Jerusalem and destruction of the city, realize it is the day of God's vengeance; it is the punishment that prophets warned would come if the people of Israel did not remain faithful to God. [23]The fall of Jerusalem is going to be a horrific, terrible period of time. How tragic it will be for pregnant women and nursing mothers, as they may be the slowest running away and be caught in the slaughter. Great misery, anguish, and distress will be released on these Israelite lands and a torrential wrath will be released on these people. [24]They will be killed with swords or dragged off as prisoners for all the world to see. These non-Jewish Romans will completely trample down Jerusalem. From then on, Jerusalem will never be a pure, dedicated city to God again. Gentiles, whom you consider to be impure, will mingle in the city's midst. They will mingle in the city until history is no more and God makes all things, including Jerusalem, new and holy again.

> 6.2.3. *The old way of religious life is ending, but it is not the end of the story; God's kingdom is coming to the world in a new way (21:25-28).*

[25]"Those are the immediate, short-term realities that are coming; they are signals to you that the end of the age is near—signals that will let you know you need always to be prepared for the end, no matter when it comes. As for what the ultimate and final end looks like, let Me tell you a few things about how it will be when God steps into human history, declares time to be no more, and brings His final judgment. Upon His decisive and final return, there will be strange cosmic occurrences in the sun, moon, and stars. All the nations of the earth will be in turmoil, perplexed by the roaring seas and strong, raging

tides that slam the earth. ²⁶When people see the powers of the heavens fully turned against the earth, they will faint with fear; they will be filled with a holy dread for what is coming upon the world. ²⁷Then you will see the One bringing divine hope and vindication arrive and take over! Everyone will see the Son of Man—the One filled with all divine power and authority—arriving on a cloud, and, with the magnificence of His power, bringing the cosmos under His control. His arrival and the display of His power will demonstrate a fullness of transcendent splendor beyond anything you can imagine. ²⁸So, when all of these cosmic, apocalyptic, truly "end times" things happen, you should raise your heads up from fear and stand strong because the victory of your ultimate salvation is at hand."

> 6.2.4. The old way of religious life is ending; one should keep their eyes open to see what God is doing and be ready for the end (21:29-38).

²⁹Then Jesus told them this parable: "To understand My point more completely, let Me give you an illustration. Look at this fig tree or any other tree. ³⁰When the leaves come out, you can readily know that summer is near and be ready for it. ³¹In the same way, when you see all these things taking place, you can know that God's rule and His kingdom is near, and you should be ready for His arrival.

³²"I tell you this truth: this generation will not pass away until all of these things happen in Jerusalem and until the time begins when every generation will need to adopt the mindset to be ready for His arrival—to be ready, at any moment in time, for the end to come. ³³And be encouraged by this fact and reality: the skies above and the earth below may pass away, but the truth of My words will never pass away; they will endure forever.

³⁴"Let Me reiterate the main point here one more time: be watchful and be ready for the end to come. Do not let the sharp readiness of your hearts be dulled by drunkenness, by behavior that is without moral constraint, or by the general concerns of daily living. If you do, then that day will surprise you just like an animal who has suddenly fallen into a trap. ³⁵Rest assured, this day is coming on everyone who lives on the face of the earth. ³⁶So, you should always be watching and

be ready at all times. Pray that you may have the strength to escape all the tragic events that are about to happen in the near future and, through your faithful endurance, be able to stand confidently before the Son of Man in His victory in the final day that is to come."

³⁷From then on, every day, Jesus was teaching at the Temple, and each evening He returned to the Mount of Olives to spend the night. ³⁸Early each morning, the crowds gathered at the Temple to listen to Jesus' teaching.

### 6.3. Recognize the betrayal of the innocent Jesus; realize His vindication is coming; and remember His teaching when His victory and vindication have been achieved (22:1–38).

#### 6.3.1. Jesus, the innocent One who is fulfilling God's plan for salvation, is betrayed (22:1–6).

## CHAPTER 22

¹Now one of the most sacred days on the Jewish calendar—the Feast of Unleavened Bread (which is also called Passover)—was approaching. This feast (the Passover) celebrated when the people of Israel were freed from their bondage in Egypt after God spared and passed over all the Jewish firstborn. It was an annual celebration recalling Israel's salvation and God's grace. ²As the time to celebrate Passover approached, the leading priests and teacher of the Jewish, Old Covenant, religious law were continually looking for some way to kill Jesus, but they feared the people's reaction if they did so. ³During this time, Satan entered into Judas Iscariot, who was one of Jesus' twelve specially appointed disciples. ⁴Apart from the others, Judas went and conferred with the executive leaders of the Jewish religion, including the leading priests and the Temple guards, who would carry out any arrest. Judas discussed with them how he could betray Jesus and give them what they needed to convict Jesus. ⁵After finalizing a plan for how they could arrest Jesus and bring Him to trial in a way that would be perceived as defending the public good, they were delighted. They agreed to pay Judas for his work and efforts. ⁶Judas agreed to the plan and the payment, and he began looking for an opportunity to betray Jesus, a time when the crowds would not be around so they could arrest Him in private.

*6.3.2. Jesus' vindication is coming; remember His sacrifice when it has been achieved (22:7–20).*

⁷Then came the day of Unleavened Bread—the day in Jewish tradition when a lamb had to be sacrificed to commemorate how, at God's direction, a lamb's sacrifice saved their firstborn from being killed during the Passover. ⁸It was customary for this four-course meal to take place within the city of Jerusalem, so Jesus sent Peter and John into the city, telling them, "Go and make preparation for us to eat the Passover meal together."

⁹They replied, "Where do you want us to go to make these preparations?"

¹⁰Jesus responded, "As you enter Jerusalem, look around. You are going to encounter a man carrying a jar of water who will greet you. Follow him back to his house. As he is about to enter his home, ¹¹say to him, 'The Teacher wants to know: Where is your guest room so that I may eat the Passover meal there with My disciples?' ¹²He will then show you a large second-story room that is already furnished and set up. That is where you should prepare the Passover meal for us."

¹³They went into the city and found everything just as Jesus had told them. They prepared the Passover meal there as instructed.

¹⁴Later that night, when the hour came for the Passover meal, Jesus and His apostles (another name for His twelve specially appointed disciples who would be entrusted to convey His message authoritatively) sat down at the table together. ¹⁵Then Jesus said to them, "It is with very deep and reverent emotion that I approach this hour. I have been very eager and looking forward to eating this Passover meal with you in these final moments before the time of My suffering begins. ¹⁶I tell you this reality: I will not eat another meal celebrating God's deliverance with you again until all things find their fulfillment in the fullness of God's kingdom that is yet to come."

¹⁷During an early portion of this four-course meal of remembrance, Jesus took a cup of wine and said, "Take this wine, share it among yourselves, and enjoy it. ¹⁸For I tell you that I will not drink and enjoy

wine again until the kingdom of God arrives."

[19]During the third course of the meal, when bread, lamb, and bitters were served, Jesus took the bread and gave thanks to God for it. He broke it into pieces and gave each of His disciples a piece of it with these instructions, "What I am giving represents My body. When you eat it, remember Me."

[20]After the supper was over, Jesus took another cup of wine and said, "This cup represents the new covenant between God and humankind—a covenant where the full forgiveness of your sins is available and a covenant that makes God accessible to you in a personal, direct way. This new covenant between God and humankind is made possible by My blood, which is poured out as a sacrifice on your behalf so that you can be made right with God.

> 6.3.3. *Jesus' vindication is coming; remember His teaching when it has been achieved (22:21–38).*

[21]"But there is also another dynamic present at this table right now: the hand of the person who will betray Me is here on the table with Mine. [22]The Son of Man will follow the path as God has determined and planned. But what divinely appointed hardship and distress awaits the person who betrays Him!" [23]Immediately, the disciples began to interrogate each other, trying to determine which one of them might be the betrayer.

[24]It was just a matter of moments before their interrogation turned into a debate about which one of the apostles was the best follower of Jesus, and who would be considered the greatest among them when God's kingdom comes. [25]To correct their incorrect thinking on how greatness was viewed in God's eyes, Jesus intervened in their discussion. He said, "In this world, kings rule over their people, and people in positions of authority like to hold the sole power of being benefactors who can decide what to give the people beneath them. [26]But greatness among My followers is not determined like that; in God's economy, greatness is measured differently. Let the one who is greatest among you see themselves as a youth who lives among elders who are more worthy of respect and service than they are. Let the one who is

the ruler or leader be like the servant of everyone else.

[27]"For who do you think is greater, the one who sits at the table and is served or the one who serves all the others sitting at the table? From a worldly perspective, we might be tempted to think it is the one who sits at the table, right? However, that is not how God views things; it is also not the way I have modeled for you. I have come and lived among you and demonstrated a life of serving others; that is the way I have modeled for you to follow.

[28]"And you have stood by Me through My trials. Do you not realize that you all will equally receive the greatest reward possible for your faithfulness? [29]Just as My Father has granted Me a kingdom, because you have faith and follow me, I will grant you a place in My kingdom. [30]As part of My kingdom, you will sit at the victory table and eat and drink with Me. And you all will be in leadership positions in the new community of My kingdom, where you will be empowered to exercise judgment over all of God's people.

[31]"Simon Peter, I want you to listen to this: Satan has asked to sift each of your faithfulness like one would sift through wheat. [32]But I have prayed for you, Simon Peter, that your faith may not fail. But after it does, and when you have turned back to Me again, be sure to strengthen and establish your brothers."

[33]Then Peter said, "Lord, I will not falter. I am ready to go to prison with you, or even to death if that is what is needed.

[34]Jesus replied, "Peter, let Me tell you something that is about to happen. Before the rooster crows tomorrow morning, you will deny that you know Me three times."

[35]Then Jesus said to them, "Do you remember in the past when I sent you out to share the good news with others and you did not have any money or a suitcase or even an extra pair of shoes? At that time, did you lack or need anything?"

They answered, "No."

³⁶Jesus said, "Well, from now on, things are going to be different. When you go out into the world, you will need to be prepared. Take your money, and take enough provisions with you for your journey. The world will be hostile to you, so if you do not have a sword to defend yourself, you may want to sell one of your coats to buy one. ³⁷I am telling you right now that what was written about Me in Isaiah 53:12 is being fulfilled: 'And He was considered a social rebel and criminal.' You must realize that everything that has been written about Me in the Scriptures must be and is about to be fulfilled."

³⁸Misunderstanding His point about needing to be prepared to encounter a hostile world and thinking they needed to be ready for a military battle, the disciples took an inventory of their swords.

They said, "See, Lord, we currently have two swords among us."

Jesus replied, "That is enough talk about swords; you have not understood My point about what your future life of faith in the world will be like and what responsibility in it will be."

### 6.4. Recognize that Jesus's innocent suffering is part of God's plan for fulfilling His plan to make salvation available to all (22:39–23:56).

#### 6.4.1. Jesus, the innocent One sent from God, prepares for His suffering through prayer (22:39–46).

³⁹After the Passover meal, as He did each evening while in Jerusalem, Jesus, followed by His disciples, returned to the Mount of Olives, which is just outside of the city. ⁴⁰When they arrived, Jesus went to pray. He told the disciples, "Pray that you will not give in to temptation when it comes." ⁴¹Then Jesus pulled away from the disciple several meters, roughly about a stone's throw away from them. He knelt down and prayed, ⁴²"Father, if you are willing, please take the cup of your wrath away from Me, the cup of suffering that I am about to be served. Yet not My will, but may whatever You desire be done." ⁴³And then an angel appeared to Jesus from the heavenly realm and strengthened Him. ⁴⁴Jesus continued praying even more earnestly than before. As Jesus prayed, He was so distressed and in such agony over what was to

come that His sweat fell to the ground like drops of blood.

⁴⁵When He rose from prayer, Jesus walked back to the disciples. He found them asleep, worn out from their grief. ⁴⁶Jesus said to them, "Why are you sleeping? You should be praying so that you will not give in to temptation when it comes."

> 6.4.2. Jesus, the innocent One sent from God, is betrayed and arrested (22:47–53).

⁴⁷While Jesus was still speaking to the disciples, a crowd approached that was led by Judas (one of the twelve disciples closest to Jesus). Judas walked over to Jesus and gave Him the common, cultural greeting of a friendly kiss. ⁴⁸Then Jesus asked him, "Judas, are you betraying the Son of Man with a sign of friendly affection?"

⁴⁹Once the other disciples saw what was happening around them, they asked, "Lord, should we use our swords and fight back?" ⁵⁰And then one of the disciples swung his sword at the servant of the high priest and struck him, cutting off his ear.

⁵¹Jesus interjected, "Stop what you are doing. There shall be no more violence!" Then Jesus touched the man's ear that had been struck, and his ear was completely healed.

⁵²Jesus said to the leading priests, the officers of the Temple guard, and the civic leaders and elders who had come out to arrest Him, "Am I leading a political rebellion, or am I a dangerous criminal that you come to get Me with swords, clubs, and deadly weapons? ⁵³Every day, I was in the Temple with you, and you did not arrest or lay hands on Me there. But this is your moment, the time when the power of darkness reigns."

> 6.4.3. Jesus, the innocent One sent from God, stands trial while His followers deny Him (22:54–71).

> 6.4.3.a. Jesus' followers deny Him (22:54-62).

⁵⁴The Temple guards arrested Jesus and lead Him away. They took Him into the house of the chief priest. Peter was following the action

from a safe distance. ⁵⁵In the middle of the large courtyard outside of the chief priest's home, they kindled a fire and sat down around it. Peter joined them around the fire. ⁵⁶Then, a servant girl noticed Peter in the firelight and stared at him. After a few moments of staring, she said, "This man is one of Jesus' followers."

⁵⁷But Peter denied the accusation, saying, "Woman, you must be crazy. I do not know Him at all."

⁵⁸A little later, someone else looked at Peter and accused him, saying, "You are one of His followers."

Peter replied, "I am not!"

⁵⁹After about an hour, another person claimed, "This guy has to be one His followers. He looks like a Galilean and has their accent."

⁶⁰But Peter replied, "Are you out of your mind? I have no idea what you are even talking about!" Immediately, while Peter was still speaking, the rooster crowed.

⁶¹From a distance away, the Lord turned and looked directly at Peter. Suddenly, Peter remembered what Jesus had told him earlier: "Before the rooster crows today, you will deny Me three times." ⁶²Then Peter left the courtyard and wept bitterly.

### 6.4.3.b. Others mock Jesus (22:63-65).

⁶³Now the guards who were holding Jesus increased their abuse. They began mocking and beating Him. ⁶⁴They blindfolded Jesus and taunted Him, saying, "Hey Prophet, give us a word of prophecy now! Tell us who is hitting You!" ⁶⁵And they continued to hurl all kinds of slanderous and horrible insults at Jesus.

### 6.4.3.c. Jesus stands trial (22:66-71).

⁶⁶When daybreak came, the assembly of the Jewish leaders in the community, which included both the leading priests and teachers of the religious law, met together. ⁶⁷They said, "Are you the Christ, the One who is to overthrow the powers of this world?" Jesus answered, "Do

you really want to know? I doubt you do; you already have your mind made up. If I told you the true answer, it would not matter. You will not believe Me. ⁶⁸If I asked you, I doubt you would tell Me the true intent of your question. ⁶⁹So, in reply to your question, here is what I will tell you: from now on, the Son of Man will be seated in the place of power at the right hand of Almighty God."

⁷⁰Then they all asked, "Are you saying that you are the Son of God, One who has direct access to be in God's presence and to be seated next to Him?"

Jesus replied, "You say that I am."

⁷¹Understanding His reply as a positive affirmation to their question, they replied, "Why do we need any more evidence? We have heard His horrendous, political, and sacrilegious blasphemy for ourselves! The convicting words came out of His own mouth!"

> 6.4.4. Jesus, the innocent One sent from God, stands trial before Pilate and Herod; His innocence is on full display (23:1–12).

## CHAPTER 23

¹Then the entire assembly of Jewish religious leaders arose and led Jesus to Pilate, the Roman governor over the region of Judea. ²Before Pilate, the Jewish religious leaders began to make their case against Jesus, saying, "We have found this man undermining law and order in our nation. He forbids us to pay taxes to the Roman government and claims to the Messiah—a King who will overthrow all worldly powers and their rule."

³So Pilate asked Jesus, "Is this true, are You the King of the Jews?"

Jesus replied, "You have said that I am."

⁴Pilate turned to the leading priests and the crowd and said, "I do not find this Man guilty of government insurrection."

⁵But they insisted, saying, "Jesus is stirring up civil unrest among all

the people of Judea and everywhere He goes through His teaching. He started out in Galilee and has now made it all the way here. He is a seriously dangerous Man who threatens to disturb our peace."

⁶Upon hearing this, Pilate asked if this Man was a Galilean. ⁷When Pilate learned that Jesus was a Galilean, that fact placed Him under the localized jurisdiction of Herod Antipas, who was the Roman official over Galilee. So, Pilate sent Jesus over to Herod, who just happened to be in Jerusalem at the time.

⁸When Herod Antipas saw Jesus, he was delighted. He had desired to see Jesus for a long time. Herod had heard of Jesus' reputation, and he was hoping to see Jesus perform a miracle. ⁹He asked Jesus many questions, but Jesus did not answer any of them. ¹⁰Meanwhile, the leading priests and teachers of the Jewish law were standing there and making vehement accusations against Jesus. ¹¹Then Herod Antipas and his soldiers began mocking and ridiculing Jesus. They also dressed Jesus in an elegant, royal robe, to mock His kingship, and sent Him back to Pilate. ¹²Before these trials of Jesus, Pilate and Herod had been enemies, yet through passing Jesus back and forth, they became friends that day.

> 6.4.5. *Jesus, the innocent One sent from God, is rejected and condemned to death instead of a person who is fully guilty; His rejection in order to fulfill God's plan of salvation has been completed (23:13–25).*

¹³Pilate called together the leading priests, Jewish civic leaders, and the crowd following them. ¹⁴He said to them, "You brought this Man to me, accusing Him of leading an insurrection against the government's law and order. I have examined Him thoroughly in front of you all. I have found this Man innocent of the charges you bring against Him. ¹⁵Herod Antipas also examined Him. Herod found Him innocent of the charges and sent Him back to us. It is clear that this Man has done nothing deserving of death. ¹⁶I will therefore have Him punished through flogging and then release Him." ¹⁷[This verse is not in older manuscripts.]

¹⁸But then the large crowd responded with a deep, loud cry from the

depths of their being: "This is not what we want. Kill Him and release Barabbas to us!" [19](Barabbas was a violent criminal who had been thrown in prison for committing murder and leading a genuine insurrection against the Roman government in the city.)

[20]Pilate, shocked by their request, tried to reason with the crowd and bargain with them. He appealed to them, desiring to release Jesus, [21]but they kept shouting, "Crucify Him! Crucify Him!"

[22]Pilate tried to reason with the crowd a third time, saying, "Why should we crucify this Man? What real crime has He committed? I have found no reason to sentence Him to death. Therefore, I will have Him punished and then release Him."

[23]But the crowd responded by shouting even louder, calling out with urgent pleas. They simply would not give up demanding that Jesus be crucified, and their voices prevailed. [24]Pilate, wanting to avoid this crowd turning into a complete riot, decided to give in and grant their demand. [25]Pilate released Barabbas, the man the crowds had asked for who had been thrown in prison for insurrection and murder. Then Pilate delivered Jesus over to have done what they desired.

> 6.4.6. *Jesus, the innocent One sent from God, is crucified and dies; His sacrifice in order to fulfill God's plan of salvation has been completed (23:26–49).*

[26]As the Roman soldiers led Jesus away to be crucified, Jesus' body was weak from lack of sleep and from severe beatings. So the soldiers seized Simon of Cyrene, who was traveling into the city from the countryside, and made him carry the cross behind Jesus as they went. [27]A large crowd, including the women who had been weeping and grieving over Him, followed Jesus on His way to be crucified. [28]Jesus turned to these women and said, "You daughters of Jerusalem, do not weep for Me, but weep for yourselves and for your children. [29]For the days are coming when you will say, 'How divinely fortunate are the barren women, the women who have never had children and whose breasts have never nursed,' because they will be able to flee this city. [30]And people will think the punishment on this city will be so bad that they will beg for death, saying, 'May the mountains fall on us to end our misery,' and

plead, 'May the hills cover us and bury us under the ground.' ³¹After all, if people can do such horrible things to the vibrant, living, green tree that is right in front of them, just imagine what terrible and tragic things will happen to the dry and lifeless tress among them who have no hope."

³²As they led Jesus out to be crucified, two other criminals were being led out to be put to death with Him. ³³When they came to the placed called the Skull, where the hill protrudes out of the ground like a skull, they crucified Him there. They also crucified the two criminals along with Jesus; one was on His right side and the other was over on His left. ³⁴Then Jesus said, "Father, please forgive them, for they do not know what they are doing." Meanwhile, the soldiers gambled and cast dice to determine who would get Jesus' clothes.

³⁵The crowd of people stood watching. The Jewish religious leaders scoffed at the scene of Jesus' crucifixion. They mocked Him, saying, "He had the power to save and heal others. If He really is the Messiah—God's Chosen One who will save all of God's people—then let Him save Himself."

³⁶The soldiers also came up to Jesus, who was supposed to be a "king", and mocked Him by offering a poor beggars' mix of cheap and sour wine blended with water. ³⁷They continued to mock Jesus, saying, "If You are supposed to be the 'King of Jews' who can save the world, then why do You not save yourself!"

³⁸In typical Roman fashion, they placed a sign listing Jesus' crime on top of the cross. The sign read: "This is the King of the Jews."

³⁹One of the criminals hanging crucified beside Jesus also hurled insults at Him, saying, "So you are supposed to be some kind of Messiah? Then prove it. Save yourself, and save us too!"

⁴⁰But the criminal being crucified on the other side rebuked the one who had mocked Jesus, saying, "Do you have no fear or reverence for God at all, even though you have been sentenced to death and will be going to meet your maker very soon? ⁴¹We deserve this punishment for our crimes, but this Man has done nothing wrong."

⁴²Then he said, "Jesus, please remember me when you come into the fullness of Your kingdom and rule."

⁴³Jesus replied, "I give you this assurance: today, you will be with Me in paradise, the place where people live in right relationship with God because they have received His forgiveness and are innocent before Him."

⁴⁴It was now approaching noon, and a darkness fell across the entire land until three in the afternoon. ⁴⁵There was a total blackout as the light from the sun was blocked from shining. Suddenly, the Temple curtain to the Holy of Holies—the curtain that separated the Holy of Holies from the rest of the Temple and symbolized how humanity was separated from direct access to God—was split right down the middle and torn in two. ⁴⁶Then Jesus cried out with a loud voice and said, "Father, My life and Spirit are in Your hands!" After Jesus had said these words from Psalm 31:5, He breathed His last.

⁴⁷The Roman official who was overseeing the crucifixions saw what had happened to Jesus. He gave praise to God and said, "Certainly this was a righteous and innocent Man!" ⁴⁸When all the people who had gathered to witness the crucifixion saw the result and Jesus' death, they were overwhelmed with grief and sorrow, and they went away. ⁴⁹But all of those who knew Jesus—along with the women who had followed Him from Galilee—stood at a distance watching all of these things.

> *6.4.7. Jesus, the innocent One sent from God, is buried; His suffering in order to fulfill God's plan of salvation has been completed (23:50-56).*

⁵⁰Also, there was a man named Joseph from the Jewish town of Arimathea. He was a member of the Sanhedrin, the Jewish ruling council, and was respected as a good and upright man. ⁵¹He disagreed with the decisions and actions of the other Jewish religious leaders. As a person faithful to God, he had been patiently looking and waiting for the arrival of God's kingdom and rule. ⁵²After Jesus' death, Joseph went to Pilate and asked if He could take care of Jesus' body.

⁵³Then Joseph took Jesus' body down from the cross, wrapped Him in a long shroud of fine cloth, and laid His body in a tomb that had been cut into the stone hillside, a tomb where no one had yet been buried. ⁵⁴Joseph did all these things fairly quickly, as it was late on Friday afternoon. It was Preparation Day, which was a time when the Jewish people made preparations for the Sabbath, which would begin at sunset on Friday.

⁵⁵The women who had traveled with Jesus from Galilee followed Joseph and saw the tomb where His body was placed. ⁵⁶Then they went home and prepared spices and ointments that they could later put on Jesus' dead body after the Sabbath was over. These women were faithful Jews, and they rested on the Sabbath, too, in obedience to the Ten Commandments.

### 6.5. Realize that through the victory of Jesus' resurrection and ascension, God fulfills His plan and makes salvation available to the world (24:1-53).

*6.5.1. Jesus' resurrection fulfills God's plan of salvation and achieves His vindication and victory (24:1-12).*

## CHAPTER 24

¹Very early on Sunday morning, the first day of the week, the women took their prepared spices to the tomb where Jesus' body had been laid. ²When they arrived, they found the stone rolled away from the tomb's entrance. ³When they walked in, they did not find Jesus' body inside the tomb. ⁴As they stood there puzzled by the situation, suddenly, two men appeared to them who were apparently more than mere human beings because their clothes radiated brilliant, supernatural light. ⁵The women were terrified by their presence, and they bowed down before these supernatural beings with their faces to the ground. But the men asked, "Why are you looking for living among the dead? ⁶Jesus is not here; He has been raised from the dead! Remember what he told you while he was still with you in Galilee, ⁷that the Son of Man must be delivered into the hands of sinful men, be crucified, and on the third day be raised to life again." ⁸Then they remembered what Jesus had said.

⁹After returning from the tomb, the women told the eleven specially appointed disciples and everyone else with them the details of what occurred at the tomb. ¹⁰It was Mary Magdalene, Joanna, Mary the mother of James, and several other women who told the eleven apostles what had happened. ¹¹But most did not believe these women; their story seemed like idle tales and total nonsense. ¹²However, Peter did not have the same reaction. Instead, he got up and ran to the tomb to check it out. Stooping over to look inside the tomb, Peter saw that the linen clothes Jesus was buried in were lying there by themselves. When Peter left the tomb and went home, he was marveling at and wondering about what had happened.

> 6.5.2. *Jesus' resurrection fulfills God's plan of salvation and delights those who follow Him and the truth of His teaching (24:13-35).*

¹³That very day, two of Jesus' followers were going to the village of Emmaus, about seven miles from Jerusalem. ¹⁴They were talking with each other about all the things that had happened. ¹⁵While they were debating these things with each other, Jesus Himself suddenly came up and began walking alongside them. ¹⁶But their eyes were kept from recognizing that it was actually Jesus.

¹⁷Jesus asked them, "What are you guys discussing and debating so intensely as you are walking along?"

They stopped in their tracks; sadness filled their faces. ¹⁸Then one of them named Cleopas replied, "Are You the only person visiting Jerusalem who does not know what happened there these past few days?"

¹⁹Jesus responded, "What kind of things happened there?"

They replied, "The things that happened to Jesus of Nazareth! He was a prophet who did was mighty in both the work He did and the words He taught before God and all the people.²⁰But the leading priests and other Jewish religious leaders conspired against Him; they delivered Him over to be condemned to death, and then they crucified him.

²¹And we had such great hopes for Him, thinking He might be the One who had come to save and redeem the people of Israel. Besides all of this, it has now been three days since these things occurred. ²²But then, today, some of the women in our group of followers brought us amazingly confusing news. Early this morning, they went to the tomb where Jesus was buried, ²³but they did not find His body there. Then they came back and shared with us that angels had appeared to them in a vision while inside the tomb and told them that Jesus was not dead but alive! ²⁴Upon hearing this news, some of our companions went out to investigate the scene at the tomb. They found it just as the women had said: Jesus' body was gone."

²⁵Then Jesus said to them, "Are you so foolish and slow of heart that you do not believe all that the prophets have spoken and what is written in the Scriptures? ²⁶Was it not clearly predicted that the Christ—the One who would deliver God's people—must suffer all these things first and then enter into His full, complete glory?" ²⁷Then, beginning with the first five books of the Old Covenant Scriptures written by Moses and continuing all the way through all the books of the Old Covenant written by the Prophets, Jesus explained to them all that the Scriptures taught concerning and referring to Himself.

²⁸By this time, they were approaching the village of Emmaus and the end of their journey. Jesus acted as if He were going to continue traveling onward. ²⁹But they strongly begged Him, "Please stay with us; it is late in the evening and the day is almost over." So Jesus went into their home to stay with them.

³⁰When Jesus was at the table with them, He took the bread, gave thanks to God for it, and began giving them pieces of it. ³¹At that moment, what had kept them from recognizing Jesus' true identity was removed. Their eyes were now opened, and they realized it was actually Jesus. Suddenly, after they recognized Him, Jesus disappeared and vanished right in front of their eyes. ³²They asked each other, "How did we not recognize it was Jesus? Did our hearts not burn with a supernatural, spiritual sense while He was talking with us on the road and as He opened up our understanding of the Old Covenant Scriptures about Himself?"

³³Astonished at what had happened on the road to Emmaus, they did not care that it was late. They got up and went back to Jerusalem. When they arrived back in the city, they found the eleven specially appointed disciples and all those gathered together with them. ³⁴These men who had been visited on the road told the eleven disciples, "All of this really has happened! The Lord has been raised from the dead. He has appeared to Simon (Peter)!" ³⁵Then the two men from Emmaus told everyone what happened on the road and how their eyes had been opened to recognizing Jesus while He was breaking bread with them during super.

> 6.5.3. *Jesus' resurrection fulfills God's plan of salvation; before He ascends, He gives a promise to hold onto and a commission that they must fulfill (24:36–53).*

³⁶As they were still discussing what had happened, Jesus suddenly appeared, standing directly in front of them, and said, "Do not be distressed any longer; divine peace is with you." ³⁷But they were startled and frightened, thinking they saw a ghost.

³⁸Then Jesus said to them, "Why are you so disturbed and troubled? Why do doubts arise in your hearts and minds? ³⁹Look at My hands and feet. You can see that it is Me! Go ahead, touch Me, and see that I am not a ghost; see that I have a physical body with flesh and bones."

⁴⁰As Jesus said these words, He showed them His hands and feet. ⁴¹They stood mesmerized by joy, marveling at the amazing wonder of what they were seeing. Then Jesus asked them, "Do you have anything to eat? If I eat something, it may help you see that I am not a ghost." ⁴²They gave Jesus a piece of broiled fish, ⁴³and He took it and ate it in front of them.

⁴⁴Then Jesus said to them, "If you recall, when I was with you before, I told you that everything written about Me in the Scriptures of the Old Covenant—from the Law of Moses to the Prophets to Psalms—must be fulfilled. And now it has been."

⁴⁵Then Jesus opened up their minds to properly understand the Scriptures of the Old Covenant. ⁴⁶He said to them, "This is God's

plan and divine design that was written in Scriptures long ago, that the Christ should suffer, that He rise from the dead on the third day, ⁴⁷and that His message—the message of how turning to trust fully in God leads to God's forgiveness of sins—will be communicated in the authority of His character to all nations, beginning first in Jerusalem. ⁴⁸You are witnesses who have seen all of these things firsthand. ⁴⁹And behold, I will send the Holy Spirit upon you to empower and guide you, just as My Father has promised. But stay here in the city of Jerusalem until this power from on high comes upon you and covers you like your clothes."

⁵⁰When Jesus led them out of the city and over to the vicinity of Bethany, Jesus lifted up His hands and asked God to show special favor on them. ⁵¹As Jesus was asking for God's special favor to be upon them, He departed from their sight and was carried into the heavenly realm of existence they could not see with their eyes. ⁵²They responded to the occasion by worshiping Him, and then they returned to the city of Jerusalem filled with great and exuberant joy. ⁵³Upon their return to Jerusalem, they were continually found spending their time in the Temple and praising God for all He had done.

www.ingramcontent.com/pod-product-compliance
Lightning Source LLC
Chambersburg PA
CBHW070610010526
**44118CB00012B/1480**